KB084750
READING
101
LEVEL
3

READING 101 Level 3

지은이 넥서스영어교육연구소
펴낸이 임상진
펴낸곳 (주)넥서스

출판신고 1992년 4월 3일 제 311-2002-2호 ⑥
10880 경기도 파주시 지목로 5
전화 (02) 330-5500 팩스 (02) 330-5555

ISBN 979-11-89432-11-9 54740
979-11-89432-08-9 (SET)

가격은 뒤표지에 있습니다.
잘못 만들어진 책은 구입처에서 바꾸어 드립니다.

www.nexusbook.com

한번에 끝내는 중등 영어 독해

READING

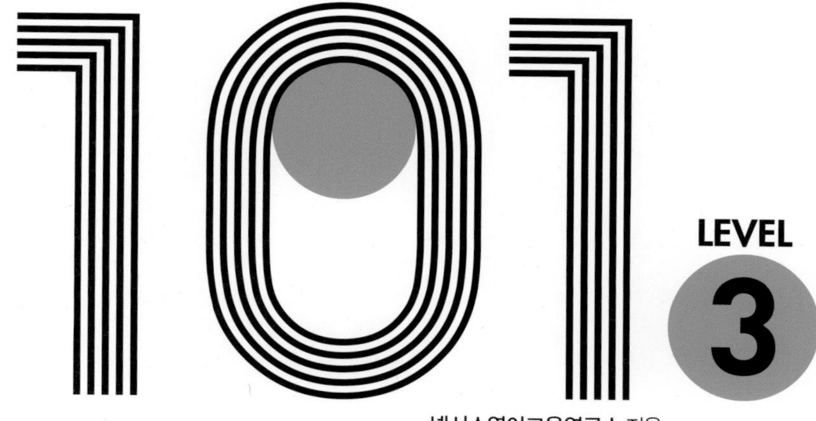

넥서스영어교육연구소 지음

NEXUS Edu

101

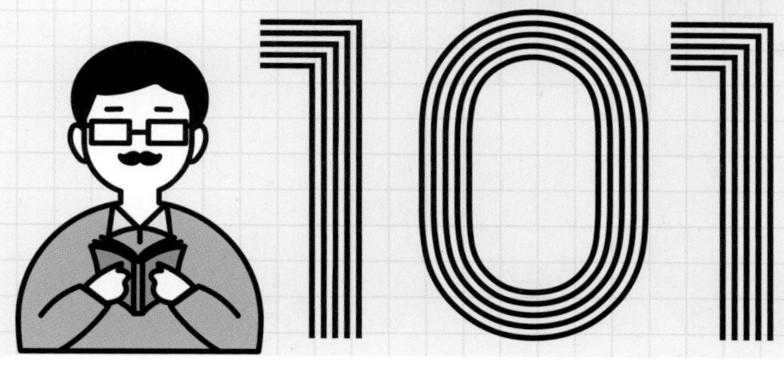

10+1가지의 특별함

1 Diverse and Fun
여행, 과학, 역사, 인물, 사회, 환경, IT 등을 바탕으로 한 다양하고 흥미로운 이야기

2 Scholastic
독해 실력 향상은 물론, 각종 실전 대비를 위한 독해유형별 5지선다형 문제풀이

3 Open-ended
내신 대비는 물론, 영어 실력을 쌓게 하는 서술형 문제풀이

4 Authentic
우리말이 아닌 영어로 의미를 정확히 파악하는 영영풀이 어휘 문제

5 Comprehensive
독해의 기본인 어휘력을 향상시키고 영작문을 최종 점검하는 유닛별 Review Test

6 Native
원어민 발음으로 이야기를 생생하게 들을 수 있는 지문 녹음 제공

7 Trained
숙련된 학습자를 만들기 위한 독해의 기본, 어휘력 강화 문제 제공(Workbook)

8 Logical
글의 흐름을 논리적으로 분석하기 위한 글의 순서 및 문장 삽입 문제 제공(Workbook)

9 Available
듣기 실력 향상은 물론 독해를 마스터할 수 있는 유용한 받아쓰기 제공(Workbook)

10 Detailed
구문 풀이를 통해 핵심 문법까지 학습할 수 있는 상세한 해설지 제공

+1 Additional
모바일 단어장, VOCA TEST, MP3 등 추가 모바일 자료 제공

1 다양한 독해 지문

총 10개 Unit, 30개의 지문으로 구성하였습니다. 다양한 주제의 글을 통해 재미있게 독해 학습을 할 수 있습니다. 글의 내용과 관련 있는 삽화를 통해 학교생활, 인문, 역사, 사회, 과학, 취미, 여행, IT등 지문의 이해력을 높여줍니다.

2 영영풀이

영단어의 의미를 영어로 정확히 파악하는 영영풀이 어휘 문제가 제공되어 영어식 사고력을 높여 줍니다.

02 FUTURE LIFE

Scientists have the ability to achieve some truly amazing things nowadays. Did you know that they can genetically modify our food? It's true. In the past, farmers have used traditional breeding techniques to grow their crops. ① They would do this by harvesting seeds from their best crops. Then, ② they would plant those seeds the next year. This method, which is used to improve the quality and the quantity of crops, is called hybridization. Even though ③ they come from their best crops, this method of breeding had many limits. ⓐ Scientists have found ways to break those limits. They can modify crops to make them ____(A)____ bacteria, viruses, and pests. ⓑ This helps to reduce the quantity of pesticides farmers use to protect ④ their crops. In addition, modifying seeds can help ⑤ them produce ____(B)____ crops. ⓒ For instance, nobody knows how safe genetically modified food really is. ⓓ There have not been any experiments designed to test the long-term effects of genetically modified food. ⓔ

*hybridization: 이종 교배(다른 종(種) 간의 교배)

영영풀이 다음 설명에 해당하는 단어를 윗글에서 찾아 넣으시오.

1 m________ to make small changes to something in order to improve it and make it more suitable or effective
2 b________ to keep animals or plants in order to produce babies or new plants, especially ones with particular qualities
3 m________ a planned way of doing something, especially one that a lot of people know about and use

86

1 윗글의 주제로 알맞은 것은? [주제 찾기]
① Alaska becoming the 49th U.S. state
② the purchase of Alaska
③ the discovery of gold in Alaska
④ the economy and people of Alaska
⑤ a meeting with President Eisenhower

2 윗글을 읽고 추론할 수 있는 것은? [내용 추론]
① Eisenhower was born in Alaska when it was a Russian state.
② Eisenhower always wanted to sign the Alaska Statehood Act.
③ Eisenhower resigned before the Alaska Statehood Act.
④ Eisenhower was considering signing the Statehood Act before meeting the delegates.
⑤ Eisenhower tried to invade Japan with the Russian military during World War II.

서술형
3 윗글을 읽고 미국인들이 알래스카를 밑줄 친 Seward's Folly와 같이 부른 이유를 영어로 쓰시오. [이유 찾기]

서술형
4 다음은 알래스카가 미국의 49번째 주가 되기까지의 과정을 정리한 것이다. 빈칸을 채우시오. [요약문 완성하기]

The United States bought Alaska from ____________ in 1867. Some years later ____________ was discovered in Alaska and during World War II, it became an important spot for strategic purposes. With these reasons, the U.S. government decided to make it the forty-ninth state. Finally, President Eisenhower signed ____________ in 1958, and Alaska became ____________ of the United States in 1959.

VOCA 101

name after ~의 이름을 따서 짓다
statehood n. 주(州)로서의 지위
strategic a. 전략적인
convince v. 확신시키다, 설득하다
insist v. 주장하다
ignore v. 무시하다
elect v. 뽑다, 선출하다
act n. 법령
purchase n. 구입 v. 구입하다
declare v. 선포하다, 공표하다
delegate n. 대표, 사절

Unit 10 89

3 시험에 꼭 나오는 문제

중·고등학교 내신과 수능에 자주 출제되는 독해 문제 유형을 쏙쏙 뽑아 실전에 대비할 수 있도록 구성했습니다. 서술형 문제를 통해 다양한 시험 대비는 물론, 영어 실력의 기본기를 탄탄히 쌓을 수 있습니다.

4 VOCA 101

지문에 나온 어려운 어휘들을 다시 정리함으로써 독해력의 기본인 어휘력을 향상 시킬 수 있습니다.

독해 지문에 쓰인 어휘의 뜻은 물론, 동의어 또는 유의어를 확인 학습할 수 있는 문제를 제공합니다. 각각의 지문에서 학습한 중요 문장들을 영작해 볼 수 있는 문제를 통해 서술형 시험에 대비할 수 있습니다.

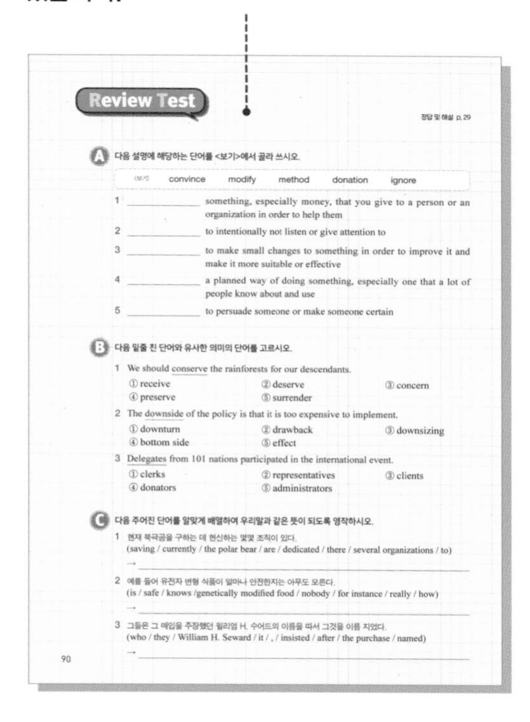

Review Test

정답 및 해설 p.29

A 다음 설명에 해당하는 단어를 <보기>에서 골라 쓰시오.

<보기> convince modify method donation ignore

1 __________ something, especially money, that you give to a person or an organization in order to help them
2 __________ to intentionally not listen or give attention to
3 __________ to make small changes to something in order to improve it and make it more suitable or effective
4 __________ a planned way of doing something, especially one that a lot of people know about and use
5 __________ to persuade someone or make someone certain

B 다음 밑줄 친 단어와 유사한 의미의 단어를 고르시오.

1 We should conserve the rainforests for our descendants.
① receive ② deserve ③ concern
④ preserve ⑤ surrender

2 The downside of the policy is that it is too expensive to implement.
① downturn ② drawback ③ downsizing
④ bottom side ⑤ effect

3 Delegates from 101 nations participated in the international event.
① clerks ② representatives ③ clients
④ donators ⑤ administrators

C 다음 주어진 단어를 알맞게 배열하여 우리말과 같은 뜻이 되도록 영작하시오.

1 현재 북극곰을 구하는 데 헌신하는 몇몇 조직이 있다.
(saving / currently / the polar bear / are / dedicated / there / several organizations / to)
→ __________

2 예를 들어 유전자 변형 식품이 얼마나 안전한지는 아무도 모른다.
(is / safe / knows /genetically modified food / nobody / for instance / really / how)
→ __________

3 그들은 그 매입을 주장했던 윌리엄 H. 수어드의 이름을 따서 그것을 이름 지었다.
(who / they / William H. Seward / it / , / insisted / after / the purchase / named)
→ __________

90

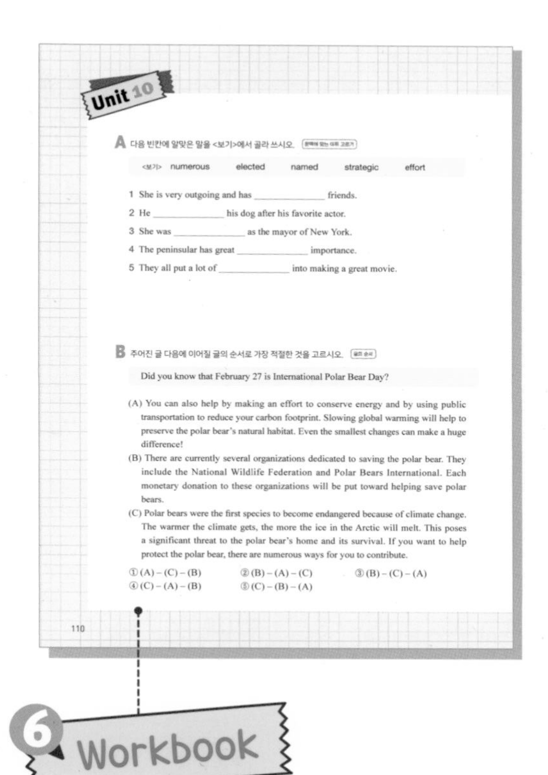

Unit 10

A 다음 빈칸에 알맞은 말을 <보기>에서 골라 쓰시오.

<보기> numerous elected named strategic effort

1 She is very outgoing and has __________ friends.
2 He __________ his dog after his favorite actor.
3 She was __________ as the mayor of New York.
4 The peninsular has great __________ importance.
5 They all put a lot of __________ into making a great movie.

B 주어진 글 다음에 이어질 글의 순서로 가장 적절한 것을 고르시오.

Did you know that February 27 is International Polar Bear Day?

(A) You can also help by making an effort to conserve energy and by using public transportation to reduce your carbon footprint. Slowing global warming will help to preserve the polar bear's natural habitat. Even the smallest changes can make a huge difference!
(B) There are currently several organizations dedicated to saving the polar bear. They include the National Wildlife Federation and Polar Bears International. Each monetary donation to these organizations will be put toward helping save polar bears.
(C) Polar bears were the first species to become endangered because of climate change. The warmer the climate gets, the more the ice in the Arctic will melt. This poses a significant threat to the polar bear's home and its survival. If you want to help protect the polar bear, there are numerous ways for you to contribute.

① (A) – (C) – (B) ② (B) – (A) – (C) ③ (B) – (C) – (A)
④ (C) – (A) – (B) ⑤ (C) – (B) – (A)

110

6 Workbook

각 Unit에 나온 지문들을 이용한 『내신+수능』에 꼭 나오는 독해 유형 문제를 추가적으로 풀어 보도록 구성했습니다. 또한, 제공되는 음원으로 본문 받아쓰기를 해 보면서 독해력은 물론 청취력까지 향상시킬 수 있습니다.

MP3 듣기

어휘 리스트
& 테스트지

모바일 단어장
& VOCA TEST

www.nexusbook.com

CONTENTS

UNIT 01
1 FESTIVALS
라 토마티나
2 PEOPLE
자신만의 예술을 창조한 예술가, 앤디 워홀
3 INTERESTING FACTS
하늘이 파랗게 보이는 이유는?

01 FESTIVALS

1 ⓐ Have you ever heard about a strange Spanish festival called La Tomatina? It is an annual food fight festival held in the town of Buñol. Each year, up to 20,000 people participate in the world's largest food fight in the streets of the town. The festival takes place on the ⓑ last Wednesday of August. It also takes place at the peak of the tomato harvesting season. In fact, nearly 140 tons of overripe tomatoes are transported into the city for the festival. Once the ceremonial rocket is fired into the air, the food fight begins. ⓒ The fight lasts for one full hour! Afterward, the streets are filled with tomato juice. Storekeepers use huge plastic covers to protect their storefronts from the huge mess. The festival is a week-long celebration that features music, parades, dancing, and fireworks. It attracts lots of tourists from all over the world. This festival gives a new meaning to the expression "______(A)______ your food."

영영풀이 다음 설명에 해당하는 단어를 윗글에서 찾아 넣으시오.

1 h______________ to gather crops from the fields
2 t______________ to take goods, people, etc. from one place to another in a vehicle
3 m______________ a dirty, untidy, or disordered condition

정답 및 해설 p. 2

1 윗글의 밑줄 친 ⓐ Have you ever heard about과 의미적 쓰임이 같은 문장은? [어법]

① Jane has lost her sunglasses.
② I've just finished writing an essay.
③ I've never been so frightened in my life.
④ Thomas has lived in Seoul since he married Yuna.
⑤ Rebecca has taught English at the middle school for three years.

2 last, lasts에 유의하여 ⓑ와 ⓒ를 해석하시오. 

ⓑ ______________________ ⓒ ______________________

3 Which of the following best fits in the blank (A)? [빈칸 완성]

① selling ② cooking ③ planting
④ fighting for ⑤ playing with

4 윗글의 내용과 일치하지 않는 것은? [내용 불일치]

① La Tomatina takes place once a year.
② Participants harvest tomatoes during La Tomatina.
③ A lot of tomatoes are used for La Tomatina.
④ People can enjoy other events including a tomato fight in La Tomatina.
⑤ La Tomatina lasts for a week.

VOCA 101

annual a. 연례의
peak n. 최고, 절정
transport v. ~을 운송하다, 수송하다
attract v. ~을 끌어 들이다
participate in ~에 참여하다
harvest v. ~을 수확하다
ceremonial a. 의식의, 기념의
expression n. 표현
take place 개최되다, 일어나다
overripe a. 너무 익은
feature v. ~을 특징으로 하다

02 PEOPLE

Andy Warhol is one of the most influential artists of the twentieth century. He was often very ill when he was a child, so he spent a lot of time drawing pictures in bed. When he got older, he studied fine art in college. He eventually moved to New York City in the 1960s, and there he began creating some of the world's best known artwork. Warhol loved popular culture. He painted large pictures of Coca-Cola bottles, Campbell's soup cans, and dollar bills. He also painted celebrities. He was one of the first painters to mass-produce their artwork. Many criticized him for turning ______(A)______ into ______(B)______. Some people were unhappy because they thought he was just making copies of the same picture, and they felt he was only interested in making money. However, Warhol believed in ______(C)______ he was doing, and he continued to create his own style of art until his death in 1987.

영영풀이 다음 설명에 해당하는 단어를 윗글에서 찾아 넣으시오.

1 p__________ relating to ordinary people, or intended for ordinary people

2 c__________ a famous living person

3 c__________ to express your disapproval of someone or something, or to talk about their faults

1 윗글의 빈칸 (A)와 (B)에 들어갈 말로 가장 적절한 것은? 빈칸 완성

(A)		(B)
① art	…	a business
② pop culture	…	large pictures
③ products	…	great fine art
④ fast food	…	popular culture
⑤ art	…	only one picture

2 윗글의 빈칸 (C)에 들어갈 말로 가장 적절한 것은? 빈칸 완성

① which ② that ③ what ④ whom ⑤ how

서술형

3 윗글에서 앤디 워홀 그림의 소재를 포괄하는 단어를 찾아 영어로 쓰시오. (2단어) 세부 사항

____

VOCA 101

influential a. 영향력이 큰, 힘 있는
popular culture n. 대중문화
criticize v. ~을 비판하다
fine art n. 미술
celebrity n. 유명인, 명사
copy n. 복사본
eventually ad. 결국
mass-produce v. ~을 대량 생산하다
continue v. 계속하다

03 INTERESTING FACTS

1 It is a common myth that the sky is blue because of a reflection of the seas and oceans. But it is not true at all. In fact, blue light from the sun spreads around much more than all the other colors from the sun. That's what causes the sky to appear blue.

5 Light is made up of electromagnetic waves, and the distance between two crests in this wave is called the wavelength. Red light, for instance, has the longest wavelength. The wavelength of blue light is about half that of red light. This difference in wavelength causes blue light to be scattered nearly ten times more than red light. Lord Rayleigh studied this phenomenon in detail, 10 and that's why it is commonly called as "Rayleigh scattering." There are some scientists, _______________, who call this "the Tyndall effect."

영영풀이 다음 설명에 해당하는 단어를 윗글에서 찾아 넣으시오.

1 r_______________ an image that you can see in a mirror, glass, or water

2 c_______________ the top or highest point of something such as a hill or a wave

3 d_______________ all the separate features and pieces of information about something

정답 및 해설 p. 3

1 윗글의 빈칸에 들어갈 알맞은 말은? (빈칸 완성)

① for example ② moreover ③ however
④ then ⑤ in addition

2 윗글의 내용과 일치하는 것은? (내용 일치)

① Light is made up of wavelengths.
② Red light spreads much more than all the other colors.
③ Red light scatters nearly ten times more than blue light.
④ The wavelength of blue light is shorter than that of red light.
⑤ The space between two parts of light waves is called electromagnetic waves.

3 윗글을 읽고 레일리 경(Lord Rayleigh)에 대해 추론할 수 있는 것은? (내용 추론)

① He was the first person to study the earth's atmosphere.
② He was the first person to understand why the sky appears blue.
③ He was the first person to find out the differences in wavelength.
④ He was the first person to study the sun's effect on our atmosphere.
⑤ He was the first person to understand the role that the sun plays in our atmosphere.

4 다음은 윗글의 내용을 요약한 것이다. 빈칸을 채우시오. (요약문 완성하기)

Although many people think that the sky is blue because of the ______________ of water, it is actually due to the length of the ______________ wavelength from the sun as it is scattered through our atmosphere.

VOCA 101

myth n. 잘못 알려진 통념; 신화
be made up of ~로 구성되다
wavelength n. 파장
in detail 상세히, 세부적으로
reflection n. 반사
electromagnetic wave n. 전자파
scatter v. 흩어지다, 흩뿌리다
effect n. 효과
ocean n. 대양
distance n. 거리
phenomenon n. 현상

정답 및 해설 p. 4

A 다음 설명에 해당하는 단어를 <보기>에서 골라 쓰시오.

〈보기〉 transport detail reflection celebrity criticize

1 ______________ all the separate features and pieces of information about something

2 ______________ a famous living person

3 ______________ to take goods, people, etc. from one place to another in a vehicle

4 ______________ to express your disapproval of someone or something, or to talk about their faults

5 ______________ an image that you can see in a mirror, glass, or water

B 다음 밑줄 친 단어와 유사한 의미의 단어를 고르시오.

1 The next conference on English education will take place in October.

① take part in ② be declared ③ be held
④ be continued ⑤ take action

2 She is one of the most influential politicians of the twenty-first century.

① active ② radical ③ inferior
④ infamous ⑤ powerful

3 My drone club is made up of five students.

① concludes ② consists ③ forms
④ includes ⑤ builds

C 다음 주어진 단어를 알맞게 배열하여 우리말과 같은 뜻이 되도록 영작하시오.

1 일단 기념 로켓이 공중으로 발사되면 푸드 파이트가 시작된다. (the food fight / is / into / once / begins / the ceremonial rocket / fired / the air)

→ ____

2 그는 침대에 누워 그림을 그리며 많은 시간을 보냈다.
(a lot of / he / bed / pictures / spent / drawing / time / in)

→ ____

3 그것이 하늘이 푸르게 보이는 이유이다. (what / blue / the sky / that's / appear / to / causes)

→ ____

UNIT 02

1. **PLACES**
   권력과 부의 상징, 베르사유
2. **ANIMALS**
   뉴질랜드에는 뱀이 없을까?
3. **TALES FROM THE WORLD**
   지혜로운 유산 상속

01 PLACES

The Palace of Versailles, built in 1624, is the royal house of France. Originally, it was only a small hunting lodge, but King Louis XIV had an enormous expansion (A) [constructed / constructing] during his reign. The Palace of Versailles became a symbol of his power. It also demonstrated the vast wealth of the Royal Court. King Louis XIV held parties at the palace. These parties distracted many of the nobles from taking responsibility for performing their duties, which allowed King Louis XIV (B) [ruling / to rule] France without any interference from ⓐ <u>them</u>. The Palace's luxuries were so expensive that a lot of money was needed to maintain the palace. ⓑ ______________, the palace also had a huge staff dedicated to serving the king and his guests. In fact, twenty-five percent of France's national income (C) [used to pay / was used to pay] for the extravagances in the palace. Now the palace is used as a National Museum, and in 1979 it was named a World Heritage Site.

*the Royal Court: 왕실, 궁정
**World Heritage Site: 세계문화유산

영영풀이 다음 설명에 해당하는 단어를 윗글에서 찾아 넣으시오.

1 d______________ to show or prove something clearly
2 v______________ extremely large
3 d______________ to give all your attention and effort to one particular thing

정답 및 해설 p. 4

1 (A), (B), (C)의 각 괄호 안에서 어법에 맞는 표현으로 가장 적절한 것은? 어법

	(A)		(B)		(C)
①	constructing	…	ruling	…	used to pay
②	constructing	…	ruling	…	was used to pay
③	constructing	…	to rule	…	was used to pay
④	constructed	…	to rule	…	was used to pay
⑤	constructed	…	to rule	…	used to pay

2 윗글에서 밑줄 친 ⓐ them이 지칭하는 것을 찾아 영어로 쓰시오. (2단어) 지칭 추론

____

3 윗글의 빈칸 ⓑ에 들어갈 말로 가장 적절한 것은? 빈칸 완성

① In spite of
② As a result
③ In addition
④ In contrast
⑤ On the other hand

VOCA 101

lodge n. 산장, 별장
demonstrate v. 보여주다, 입증하다
luxury n. 사치품, 사치
extravagance n. 사치, 낭비
enormous a. 거대한, 막대한
distract v. (마음 · 주의를) 흐트러뜨리다
dedicate v. 헌신하다
reign n. 재위 기간
interference n. 방해, 간섭
income n. 수입

02 ANIMALS

1 Are you afraid of snakes? If so, you might want to consider ⓐ relocating to New Zealand. This island in the South Pacific Ocean is completely free of land snakes. ______(A)______, the island has only a small number of indigenous animals ⓑ included bats, lizards, and frogs. For millions of years, New Zealand 5 was isolated, which allowed many unique species of animals ⓒ to thrive on the island. For example, a shy and flightless bird called kiwi is one of New Zealand's best-known ⓓ inhabitants. When European settlers arrived on the island, they brought many species of animals with (B) them, such as dogs, deer, rabbits, pigs, and mice. Among them, a few have seriously impacted 10 New Zealand's ecosystem, ⓔ driving many other species to extinction. ______(C)______, the kiwi, which once numbered in the millions, is now an endangered species. To protect the indigenous animals, the authorities in New Zealand impose strict regulations on the import of animals, and there are heavy penalties for illegally 15 importing any plants or animals into New Zealand.

영영풀이 다음 설명에 해당하는 단어를 윗글에서 찾아 넣으시오.

1 i__________ without much contact with other people or other countries

2 a__________ the people or an organization who have the power to make decisions or who have a particular area of responsibility in a country or region

3 i__________ to force somebody/something to have to deal with something that is difficult or unpleasant

정답 및 해설 p. 5

1 What is the best title of the passage? [제목 찾기]

① New Zealand: A Good Place to Live
② Reasons for No Snakes in New Zealand
③ History of Indigenous People in New Zealand
④ How to Raise Animals in New Zealand
⑤ The Indigenous Animals of New Zealand

2 윗글의 빈칸 (A)와 (C)에 들어갈 말로 가장 적절한 것은? [빈칸 완성]

	(A)		(C)
①	However	…	In addition
②	In fact	…	For instance
③	Therefore	…	On the other hand
④	In addition	…	Furthermore
⑤	In spite of	…	In contrast

3 What does (B) them refer to? [지칭 추론]

____

4 윗글의 ⓐ ~ ⓔ 중, 어법상 틀린 것은? [어법]

① ⓐ　② ⓑ　③ ⓒ　④ ⓓ　⑤ ⓔ

VOCA 101

relocate v. 이동하다
thrive v. 번성하다
ecosystem n. 생태계
endangered species n. 멸종 위기 종
penalty n. 벌금
indigenous a. 토착의
flightless a. 날 수 없는
extinction n. 멸종
impose v. 부과하다
import v. 수입하다
isolated a. 고립된
impact v. 영향을 미치다
number v. (수가 총) ~이다
regulation n. 규율, 규칙

03 TALES FROM THE WORLD

1 There was a chief living in Dagomba. He was very rich and had many servants and slaves. According to (A) <u>the traditions of those times</u>, a man's possessions were not given to his son. Instead they were given to his nephew. The chief wondered if his nephew would take good care of the possessions.
5 As the chief's life was ending, he told his nephew, "When I am dead, select one thing that I own and take it. Everything else I will leave to my head slave. He has been very loyal and faithful to me all my life. I want you to inherit thoughtfully." The nephew thought at first, "My uncle rejects me, so I want nothing from him at all." His mother, however, told him that perhaps there was
10 (B) <u>some meaning</u> in it that he did not understand.

After his uncle's death, the nephew asked only for the head slave and gave him a field and a house.

영영풀이 다음 설명에 해당하는 단어를 윗글에서 찾아 넣으시오.

1 p__________ something that you own or have with you at a particular time
2 i__________ to receive money, property, etc. from someone after they have died
3 r__________ to refuse to accept, use, or believe something or someone

정답 및 해설 p. 6

1 윗글의 밑줄 친 (A)가 의미하는 것은? 의미 추론

① A man's fields should be given to the town.
② A man has to plan his will.
③ A man's nephew should marry the man's daughter.
④ A man's possessions are given to his nephew.
⑤ A man's head slave has to be loyal and faithful.

2 윗글의 밑줄 친 (B)에 담긴 의미로 알맞은 것은? 의미 파악

① The chief hated his nephew.
② The chief couldn't say anything.
③ The chief wanted his head slave to inherit his possessions.
④ The chief wanted his nephew to be wise.
⑤ The chief didn't want to give all the property to his nephew.

3 윗글을 읽고 다음과 같은 내용을 추론할 수 있다. 빈칸에 알맞은 말을 고르시오. 내용 추론

Actually, all of the chief's possessions will be given to ____________.

① the head slave ② his son ③ his nephew
④ his mother ⑤ nobody

VOCA 101

chief n. 족장, 우두머리
according to ~에 따르면
loyal a. 충성스러운, 성실한
thoughtfully ad. 잘 생각해서
servant n. 하인
possession n. 재산, 소유물
faithful a. 성실한, 충실한
reject v. 버리다, 거절하다
slave n. 노예
own v. 소유하다
inherit v. 상속하다, 물려받다
ask for 요구하다

Review Test

정답 및 해설 p. 6

A 다음 설명에 해당하는 단어를 <보기>에서 골라 쓰시오.

〈보기〉 dedicate vast isolated inherit possession

1 ______________ to receive money, property, etc. from someone after they have died

2 ______________ extremely large

3 ______________ something that you own or have with you at a particular time

4 ______________ without much contact with other people or other countries

5 ______________ to give all your attention and effort to one particular thing

B 다음 밑줄 친 단어와 유사한 의미의 단어를 고르시오.

1 Rachel has been under an <u>enormous</u> amount of stress lately.

① anonymous ② ignorant ③ primary
④ immense ⑤ insignificant

2 Kangaroos are <u>indigenous</u> to Australia.

① alien ② inaccessible ③ populous
④ familiar ⑤ native

3 Wanting to travel for a year, she <u>rejected</u> the job offer.

① regretted ② took over ③ accepted
④ turned down ⑤ brought up

C 다음 주어진 단어를 알맞게 배열하여 우리말과 같은 뜻이 되도록 영작하시오.

1 궁에는 왕과 왕의 손님의 시중을 드는 데 종사하는 엄청난 수의 시종도 있었다.
(the king / a huge staff / and / the palace / serving / also / his guests / had / dedicated to)

→ ____

2 어떠한 식물이나 동물을 뉴질랜드에 불법적으로 들여오는 것에 대해 엄중한 처벌이 있다. (New Zealand / heavy penalties / into / are / illegally importing / for / any plants / there / or animals)

→ ____

3 족장은 자신의 조카가 재산을 잘 관리할지 궁금했다.
(if / take good care of / the chief / would / the possessions / wondered / his nephew)

→ ____

UNIT 03

01 ART

1 Following the Second World War, a new form of art began to emerge. It was called minimalism. This term refers to artwork ⓐ that emphasizes extreme simplicity of form by using essential elements. For instance, minimalist artists use only a few colors in their paintings. Another feature of this type of artwork can be seen in its appearance. Many minimalist painters use ______(A)______ geometric designs, such as squares or rectangles. Frank Stella was one of the first artists who used minimalist concepts in their artwork. Several of his paintings are nothing more than stripes on a canvas. Minimalism can be found in many other forms of art as well. This includes music, literature, architecture, and even philosophy. Minimalist musicians use only ______(B)______ melodies and rhythms in their songs, and the songs often contain many repetitive elements. Minimalism continued through the seventies and made a great impact on postmodern art.

영영풀이 다음 설명에 해당하는 단어를 윗글에서 찾아 넣으시오.

1 t______________ a word or expression with a particular meaning, especially one that is used for a specific subject or type of language

2 e______________ to say strongly or show clearly that a fact is especially important

3 e______________ connected with the most important aspect or basic nature of somebody/something

1 윗글의 밑줄 친 ⓐ that과 쓰임이 같은 것은? [어법]

① He probably didn't hear the news that she's moving soon.
② The girl that we saw at the bus stop is my classmate.
③ My old friend that lives in Japan called me last night.
④ He knew that she didn't know the truth.
⑤ I bought that bicycle two weeks ago.

2 윗글의 빈칸 (A)와 (B)에 공통으로 들어갈 말로 가장 적절한 것은? [빈칸 완성]

① complicated ② smooth ③ various ④ warlike ⑤ simple

3 다음 중 미니멀리즘의 그림으로 볼 수 있는 것은? [세부 사항]

① 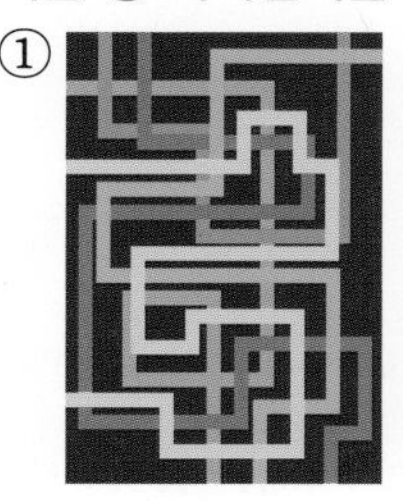
② 
③ 
④ 
⑤ 

서술형

4 윗글에서 미니멀리즘 음악의 특징 두 가지를 찾아 우리말로 쓰시오. [세부 사항]

____

VOCA 101

following prep. ~에 이어서
geometric a. 기하학의
architecture n. 건축, 건축 양식
repetitive a. 반복적인
emerge v. 나타나다, 나오다
concept n. 개념
philosophy n. 철학
postmodern a. 포스트모던(탈근대주의)의
emphasize v. 강조하다
include v. ~을 포함하다
contain v. 담다

02 SPECIAL DAYS

1

(A)

My grandfather was a veteran of the Second World War. He survived many battles, but he had to watch many of his friends die in combat. Although he used to tell me that he
5
was very proud of the service he provided for his country, he looked moody ⓐ when Memorial Day arrived each year. Since the year my grandfather passed away, I have observed this holiday alone. Whenever I attend the memorial service in my hometown, I miss him terribly.

(B)

10

In the United States, Memorial Day is a somber holiday for all to honor the men and women who sacrificed their lives defending their country. Each year cities around the U.S. organize special
15
ceremonies, parades, festivals, and other events to mark the occasion. The services honor all those who died in defense of the U.S. Memorial Day began to be celebrated after the American Civil War, and it is now observed nationwide.

영영풀이 다음 설명에 해당하는 단어를 윗글에서 찾아 넣으시오.

1 c__________ fighting or a fight, especially during a time of war
2 o__________ to arrange for something to happen or to be provided
3 d__________ the act of protecting somebody/something from attack, etc.

정답 및 해설 p. 7

1 윗글 (A)의 상황에 나타난 분위기로 가장 적절한 것은? 글의 어조

① nostalgic ② exciting ③ frightening
④ boring ⑤ nervous

2 윗글 (A)의 밑줄 친 ⓐ when과 쓰임이 같은 것은? 어법

① When do you feel homesick?
② Do you know when he will come?
③ It was early morning when we met each other.
④ I broke my wrist when I was in the sixth grade.
⑤ January 1st is the day when my first niece was born.

3 윗글 (B)의 형식으로 가장 적절한 것은? 글의 종류

① 설명문 ② 논설문 ③ 일기 ④ 편지 ⑤ 기사

4 윗글의 내용과 일치하지 않는 것은? 내용 불일치

① The grandfather was a soldier in the Second World War.
② Many of the grandfather's friends were killed in combat.
③ The grandfather wasn't proud of what he had done during the war.
④ Memorial Day is a sad holiday in the U.S.
⑤ Memorial Day started to be observed after the American Civil War.

VOCA 101

veteran n. 참전 용사
pass away 죽다
somber a. 우울한
occasion n. 행사
combat n. 전투
observe v. ~을 기념하다; ~을 보다
sacrifice v. 희생하다
defense n. 방위, 방어
moody a. 침울한
attend v. ~에 참석하다
mark v. ~을 기념하다

03 ANIMALS

1 (A) People all around the world have loved rhino horns for more than 1,000 years. Many people in Africa, Europe, Arab, China, and India have hunted a rhino to use its horn. (B) The horns were used to make status symbols and powerful medicines. In Africa some tribes used rhino horns as weapons,
5 a tool, and a good luck charm. (C) Europeans started to become interested in rhino horns in the 19th century. They used them to make the tops of walking sticks and door handles. (D) Today, it is illegal to use rhino horns to make anything. In Yemen, an Arab country, rich people have used rhino horns for short knives for centuries. And in China, rhino horns are still used to this day
10 in medicines. (E) Although all rhino species face the threat of extinction in the wild, people still desire their horns.

영영풀이 다음 설명에 해당하는 단어를 윗글에서 찾아 넣으시오.

1 w__________ something that you use to fight with or attack someone with, such as a knife, bomb, or gun

2 e__________ a situation in which something no longer exists

3 d__________ to want something very much

정답 및 해설 p. 8

1 윗글의 밑줄 친 (A) ~ (E) 중 글의 흐름과 어울리지 않는 것은? [무관한 문장 찾기]

① (A) ② (B) ③ (C) ④ (D) ⑤ (E)

2 윗글의 내용과 일치하지 않는 것은? [내용 불일치]

① The Chinese have used rhino horns in medicines.
② Some African tribes used rhino horns as medicines.
③ Europeans became interested in rhino horns from the 19th century.
④ Many people including Africans, Arabs, and Indians have wanted rhino horns.
⑤ Rhino horns were used for making the tops of walking sticks in Europe.

3 윗글의 바로 뒤에 올 내용으로 가장 알맞은 것은? [내용 추론]

① People should stop hunting rhinos.
② The governments should raise lots of rhinos to meet people's needs.
③ Besides horns, there are a lot of benefits people can get from rhinos.
④ Rhinos are really big and it's dangerous to make them angry.
⑤ People should hunt other animals except rhinos.

4 다음은 윗글의 내용을 요약한 것이다. 빈칸을 채우시오. [요약문 완성하기]

A(n) ____________________ serves many uses and has been in demand by many people from around the world for more than a millennium.

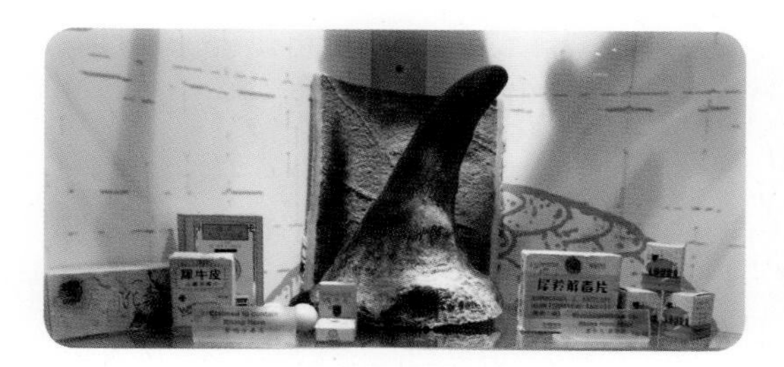

VOCA 101

rhino n. 코뿔소
weapon n. 무기
face v. 직면하다
horn n. 뿔
charm n. 부적
threat n. 위협
tribe n. 부족, 종족
illegal a. 불법인

정답 및 해설 p. 9

A 다음 설명에 해당하는 단어를 <보기>에서 골라 쓰시오.

〈보기〉 essential extinction emphasize weapon defense

1 ______________ a situation in which something no longer exists

2 ______________ something that you use to fight with or attack someone with, such as a knife, bomb, or gun

3 ______________ connected with the most important aspect or basic nature of somebody/something

4 ______________ the act of protecting somebody/something from attack, etc.

5 ______________ to say strongly or show clearly that a fact is especially important

B 다음 밑줄 친 단어와 유사한 의미의 단어를 고르시오.

1 The full moon emerged from behind the mountain.

① appeared ② emitted ③ merged
④ disappeared ⑤ reduced

2 Rob was so depressed that he didn't go out for a month after his father passed away.

① left ② panicked ③ died
④ failed ⑤ stopped by

3 This new car has all the options that you have desired.

① longed for ② purchased ③ possessed
④ observed ⑤ experienced

C 다음 주어진 단어를 알맞게 배열하여 우리말과 같은 뜻이 되도록 영작하시오.

1 그의 몇몇 그림은 캔버스에 단지 줄을 쭉쭉 그은 것에 지나지 않는다.
(than / on a canvas / are / nothing / his paintings / stripes / several of / more)

→ ____

2 고향마을에서 추모 기념식에 참석할 때마다 나는 할아버지가 너무 그립다.
(terribly / I / I / him / attend / in my hometown / miss / the memorial service / whenever)

→ ____

3 부자들은 수백 년 동안 코뿔소의 뿔로 단검을 만들었다.
(for / for / used / people / rhino horns / rich / short knives / have / centuries)

→ ____

UNIT 04
1 PLACES
마카오를 중국에 반환하다
2 TRAGEDY
911 비극의 날
3 INTERESTING FACTS
소의 트림에 지구가 위험하다

01 PLACES

1 Macau is a special administrative region of the People's Republic of China. The Macau Peninsula is located to the west of Hong Kong and ⓐ included the small islands of Taipa and Coloane. Its civilization ⓑ has existed for over 6,000 years.

(A)

However, they eventually agreed to return the colony to the People's Republic of China. On December 20, 1999, Portugal agreed to relinquish control of Macau. It is presently considered a part of China, but it also enjoys a high degree of autonomy in ⓒ many of its political matters.

(B)

This post allowed merchants ⓓ to open important trade relations between China and the Western world. The Portuguese ⓔ considered Macau to be an overseas province for a long period of time.

(C)

However, when the Portuguese arrived in the sixteenth century, they made Macau their colony in the far East. Merchant ships used it (a) as a trading outpost for various goods.

*the People's Republic of China: 중화인민공화국

영영풀이 다음 설명에 해당하는 단어를 윗글에서 찾아 넣으시오.

1 e________ at the end of a period of time or a series of events

2 c________ a country or an area that is governed by people from another, more powerful, country

3 p________ one of the areas that some countries are divided into with its own local government

정답 및 해설 p. 10

1 윗글 (A), (B), (C)의 순서로 가장 적절한 것은? [글의 순서 정하기]

① (A) – (C) – (B)　② (B) – (A) – (C)　③ (B) – (C) – (A)
④ (C) – (A) – (B)　⑤ (C) – (B) – (A)

2 윗글의 ⓐ ~ ⓔ 중, 어법상 틀린 것은? [어법]

① ⓐ　② ⓑ　③ ⓒ　④ ⓓ　⑤ ⓔ

3 윗글의 밑줄 친 (a) as와 같은 의미로 쓰인 것은? [어법]

① I'll take that as a compliment.
② As you know, I'm quite busy these days.
③ He tried to solve that problem as hard as you did.
④ We decided to go to the movies as it stopped raining.
⑤ As time passed by, he could understand what the teacher said.

4 윗글에서 다음 설명에 해당하는 단어를 찾아 영어로 쓰시오. (1단어) [어휘]

a person that buys and sells goods, especially one that trades with other countries

____

VOCA 101

administrative a. 행정상의
exist v. 존재하다
autonomy n. 자치
outpost n. 전초기지
peninsula n. 반도
colony n. 식민지
overseas a. 외국의
civilization n. 문명
relinquish v. (권리를) 양도하다
province n. (행정 구역으로서의) 주(州)

02 TRAGEDY

Do you know what happened in the United States on September 11, 2001? Four planes were hijacked by terrorists, and two of those planes hit the Twin Towers of the World Trade Center in New York City. Every passenger on board the two airplanes ____(A) kill____. A third plane was flown into the Pentagon. Some brave passengers on a fourth plane managed to overpower the hijackers before crashing into a field in Pennsylvania.

That day, everyone was glued to their television screens as the incidents took place. Osama Bin Laden was identified as the man who ordered these attacks. Soon after, President George W. Bush declared a war on terrorism. Actually, these suicide attacks ____(B) kill____ almost three thousand innocent people. All nineteen hijackers, Middle Eastern religious fanatics, were also killed. Americans felt a large amount of anger and sadness after the tragedy.

In an effort to memorialize, they started to construct a new building on the same site where the Twin Towers used to stand and opened the building in 2014. The new building, which has 104 floors, is now called One World Trade Center and is a symbol of hope and victory for not only U.S. citizens but also peace-loving people around the world.

*war on terrorism: 테러와의 전쟁 **religious fanatic: 종교적 광신도

영영풀이 다음 설명에 해당하는 단어를 윗글에서 찾아 넣으시오.

1 i____________ something that happens, especially something unpleasant
2 s____________ the act of killing yourself intentionally
3 t____________ a very sad situation, especially one involving death or suffering

정답 및 해설 p. 10

1 What is the best title of the passage? [제목 찾기]

① Vicious Attacks on September 11
② The Person Who Destroyed the Twin Towers
③ The People Who Survived on September 11
④ The War on Terrorism in the United States
⑤ Reconstruction of the World Trade Center

2 윗글의 빈칸 (A)와 (B)에 주어진 동사 kill을 어법에 맞도록 고쳐 쓰시오. [어법]

(A) ________________ (B) ________________

3 윗글의 내용과 일치하는 것은? [내용 일치]

① Four airplanes crashed into the World Trade Center.
② On the fourth plane, the passengers were killed by hijackers.
③ Some of the hijackers were caught after the attack.
④ Many people watched the World Trade Center attacked by hijackers on TV.
⑤ One of the hijackers on the plane was Osama Bin Laden.

4 윗글에서 다음 설명에 해당하는 단어를 찾아 영어로 쓰시오. (1단어) [어휘]

a person who is traveling in a motor vehicle, airplane, train, etc. but is not driving it

____

VOCA 101

hijack v. (차량, 비행기를) 납치하다
overpower v. ~을 제압하다
incident n. 사건
suicide n. 자살
in an effort to ~해보려는 노력으로
on board 탑승한
crash v. 충돌하다
identify v. (신원을) 확인하다
innocent a. 무고한
memorialize v. 기념[추모]하다
manage v. 간신히 해내다
be glued to ~에 열중하다
declare v. ~을 선언하다
tragedy n. 비극
citizen n. 시민

03 INTERESTING FACTS

1 A cow burps about 280 liters of methane every day. That doesn't seem very important to us, but the methane ⓐ what cows burp up is dangerous for our environment. Methane is a greenhouse gas, and global warming is ⓑ related to greenhouse gases. In the United States alone, every year about six million 5 tons of cows' methane go up toward the sky. Around the world, this number increases up to 80 million tons, ⓒ when sheep, goats and buffalos are included. Carbon dioxide is the major greenhouse gas, but methane is 21 times ⓓ more effective at trapping heat in the atmosphere.

The bottom line: Every time a cow belches, it is contributing to global warming 10 and the ⓔ melting of the polar ice caps.

영영풀이 다음 설명에 해당하는 단어를 윗글에서 찾아 넣으시오.

1 b__________ to pass gas loudly from your stomach out through your mouth
2 t__________ to prevent something such as gas or water from getting away
3 c__________ to help to make something happen

정답 및 해설 p. 11

1 윗글의 ⓐ ~ ⓔ 중, 어법 상 틀린 것은? [어법]

① ⓐ ② ⓑ ③ ⓒ ④ ⓓ ⑤ ⓔ

2 윗글의 밑줄 친 belches와 바꿔 쓸 수 있는 말은? [어휘]

① smells ② drifts ③ traps ④ contributes ⑤ burps

3 윗글의 내용과 일치하지 않는 것은? [내용 불일치]

① Methane is a greenhouse gas.
② Cows' burps lead to an increase of carbon dioxide.
③ Global warming is related to greenhouse gases.
④ Methane is very effective at trapping heat in the atmosphere.
⑤ In the U.S., cows produce about six million tons of methane gas every year.

4 다음은 윗글의 내용을 요약한 것이다. 빈칸에 공통으로 들어갈 말을 쓰시오. [요약문 완성하기]

The ______________ that cows burp up is dangerous for our environment. Cows, along with other livestock, burp ______________ every day and this affects global warming in the atmosphere in a negative way.

VOCA 101

burp v. 트림하다
global warming n. 지구온난화
effective a. 효과적인
contribute to ~에 기여하다
methane n. 메탄
buffalo n. 물소, 들소
trap v. (흐름을) 막다, 잡다
melt v. 녹이다
greenhouse gas n. 온실가스
carbon dioxide n. 이산화탄소
atmosphere n. 대기
polar a. 극지의

Review Test

정답 및 해설 p. 12

A 다음 설명에 해당하는 단어를 <보기>에서 골라 쓰시오.

〈보기〉 eventually contribute colony incident tragedy

1 ______________ to help to make something happen

2 ______________ a very sad situation, especially one involving death or suffering

3 ______________ a country or an area that is governed by people from another, more powerful, country

4 ______________ something that happens, especially something unpleasant

5 ______________ at the end of a period of time or a series of events

B 다음 밑줄 친 단어와 유사한 의미의 단어를 고르시오.

1 He was forced to relinquish his position as president.

① give up ② undertake ③ retain
④ maintain ⑤ abuse

2 The government declared war on drugs and crime.

① acclaimed ② denied ③ announced
④ cleared ⑤ fought

3 The terrorists have attacked more than ten major cities in Europe.

① extreme ② popular ③ limited
④ political ⑤ main

C 다음 주어진 단어를 알맞게 배열하여 우리말과 같은 뜻이 되도록 영작하시오.

1 포르투갈 사람들은 오랫동안 마카오를 자국의 국외 영토로 간주했다. (to be / a long period of time / the Portuguese / an overseas province / considered / Macau / for)

→ ____

2 오사마 빈 라덴이 이 공격을 명령한 인물로 규명되었다.
(who / was / these attacks / Osama Bin Laden / the man / identified / ordered / as)

→ ____

3 소가 트림하면서 내는 메탄은 우리 환경에 위험한 요소이다.
(the methane / our environment / burp up / that / for / dangerous / cows / is)

→ ____

UNIT 05
① CAMPAIGN
불평은 이제 그만!
② FUTURE LIFE
우주에서 휴가를 보낼 날이 올까?
③ WORLD NEWS
사라져가는 언어들

01 CAMPAIGN

How often do you complain about problems in your life?

(A)

However, if you complain, gossip about, or criticize someone, then you must move the bracelet onto your other wrist and start all over again. So stop complaining! You just might feel better about yourself.

(B)

It's a very simple idea, and it may change your life! Several researchers believe that it takes twenty-one days ______ ⓐ ______. To begin the experiment, wear a purple wristband on your right wrist. Your goal is to be wearing it on the same wrist for twenty-one days.

(C)

If you're like most people, you probably complain about your problems on a daily basis. A lot of people find ⓑ it easier to complain than try to fix them. Does this sound like you? Then you should do some research on the Complaint-Free World Project.

영영풀이 다음 설명에 해당하는 단어를 윗글에서 찾아 넣으시오.

1 c______ to say that something is wrong or not satisfactory

2 g______ to talk about other people's behavior and private lives, often including remarks that are unkind or untrue

3 d______ happening on or relating to every day

정답 및 해설 p. 12

1 윗글 (A), (B), (C)의 순서로 가장 적절한 것은? [글의 순서 정하기]

① (A) – (C) – (B)　② (B) – (A) – (C)　③ (B) – (C) – (A)
④ (C) – (A) – (B)　⑤ (C) – (B) – (A)

2 윗글의 빈칸 ⓐ에 들어갈 말로 가장 적절한 것은? [빈칸 완성]

① to find complaint　② to criticize someone
③ to break a bad habit　④ to change one's bracelet
⑤ to receive a purple wristband

3 윗글을 읽고, 빈칸 (A)와 (B)에 들어갈 말로 가장 적절한 것을 고르시오. [요약문 완성하기]

> The purpose of wearing the bracelet is to create a ___(A)___ change in our lives by ___(B)___ needless complaints.

	(A)		(B)
①	positive	…	eliminating
②	negative	…	adding
③	positive	…	criticizing
④	negative	…	reducing
⑤	dramatic	…	starting

4 윗글에서 밑줄 친 ⓑ it이 의미하는 것을 찾아 영어로 쓰시오. (2단어) [지칭 추론]

____

VOCA 101

complain v. 불평하다
experiment n. 실험
fix v. ~을 고치다
gossip v. 험담하다
wristband n. 밴드, 팔찌
do research on ~에 대해 연구하다
bracelet n. 팔찌
on a daily basis 매일

02 FUTURE LIFE

1 After the first person landed on the Moon in 1969, people began to wonder how space travel would change our lives. Would people live on the Moon? When could the average person travel into space? Well,
5 nobody lives on the Moon, yet. ⓐ But people are finally beginning to travel into space. Space tourism is a new phenomenon which is growing very quickly. ⓑ It gives people an opportunity to travel into space. ____(A)____, those opportunities are very expensive right now. ⓒ The cost of traveling into space as a passenger on a spaceship is almost thirty-five million dollars. ⓓ Likewise,
10 the cost of traveling on a cruise ship has risen sharply. ⓔ However, some companies want to start creating spaceships that can take tourists into space less expensively. New space stations are being built. There have even been attempts to begin building a hotel in space! ____(B)____, it may still take a long time before the average person can afford to take his or her vacation in the
15 stars.

영영풀이 다음 설명에 해당하는 단어를 윗글에서 찾아 넣으시오.

1 p________ something that happens or exists in society, science, or nature, especially something that is studied because it is difficult to understand

2 o________ a chance to do something or an occasion when it is easy for you to do something

3 a________ an act of trying to do something, especially something difficult

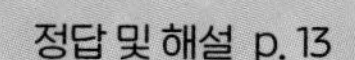

정답 및 해설 p. 13

1 윗글의 빈칸 (A)와 (B)에 공통으로 들어갈 말로 가장 적절한 것은? 빈칸 완성

① Unfortunately ② Finally ③ Luckily ④ Soon ⑤ Suddenly

2 윗글의 ⓐ ~ ⓔ 중, 글의 흐름과 관계없는 문장은? 무관한 문장 찾기

① ⓐ ② ⓑ ③ ⓒ ④ ⓓ ⑤ ⓔ

3 윗글의 내용과 일치하지 않는 것은? 내용 불일치

① A human being already visited the Moon.
② New space stations are under construction.
③ The cost of traveling into space is enormous.
④ People might be able to stay at a hotel in space in the future.
⑤ Before long, common people will be able to travel into space.

서술형

4 윗글의 제목으로 알맞은 것을 찾아 영어로 쓰시오. (2단어) 제목 찾기

____

VOCA 101

land on ~에 착륙하다
passenger n. 승객
attempt n. 시도
average a. 보통의
spaceship n. 우주선
afford v. ~할 여유가 있다
opportunity n. 기회
sharply ad. 급격하게, 큰 폭으로

03 WORLD NEWS

(A)

An endangered language is a language with nearly no one who speaks only that language. Endangered languages belong to endangered minority cultures. Cultures are best passed on to following generations through their languages, and cultures are lost when their languages are lost. Sadly, thousands of languages have already disappeared, and they are disappearing more quickly, now. About 50% of the world's languages face extinction. Many scholars worry that 90% of them will probably disappear at a rate of two languages a month.

(B)

There are around 6,800 different languages all around the world. Almost half of these languages, however, are disappearing as a result of the loss of the cultures that speak them. What are these endangered languages and why do they disappear?

(C)

What contributes to the loss of a language? Reasons such as these: the growth of cities, worldwide communication, and westernization, discrimination, starvation, and so on. These make people who belong to small communities feel ashamed to pass on their languages. Also, many people believe that children speaking a majority language have a better opportunity for future success.

영영풀이 다음 설명에 해당하는 단어를 윗글에서 찾아 넣으시오.

1 g______________ all people of about the same age
2 s______________ suffering or death caused by lack of food
3 a______________ feeling very sorry and embarrassed because of something you have done

1 윗글 (A), (B), (C)의 순서로 가장 적절한 것은? [글의 순서 정하기]

① (A) - (C) - (B)
② (B) - (A) - (C)
③ (B) - (C) - (A)
④ (C) - (A) - (B)
⑤ (C) - (B) - (A)

2 윗글에서 언어 소멸의 직접적 원인으로 언급하지 <u>않은</u> 것은? [내용 불일치]

① discrimination
② difficulty of old languages
③ westernization
④ starvation
⑤ the growth of cities

3 윗글의 내용으로 볼 때, 다음 빈칸에 들어갈 수 있는 말은? [세부 사항]

> We can say that ______________ of the world's languages are in danger of disappearing.

① a quarter ② a half ③ most ④ 6,800 ⑤ a couple

4 다음은 소멸 위기에 처한 언어에 대한 정의이다. 빈칸에 공통으로 들어갈 말을 쓰시오 [요약문 완성하기]

> A(n) ______________ language is one that is likely to become extinct in the near future. It belongs to ______________ minority cultures. Some reasons of the loss of a language are the growth of cities, worldwide communication, westernization, discrimination, and starvation.

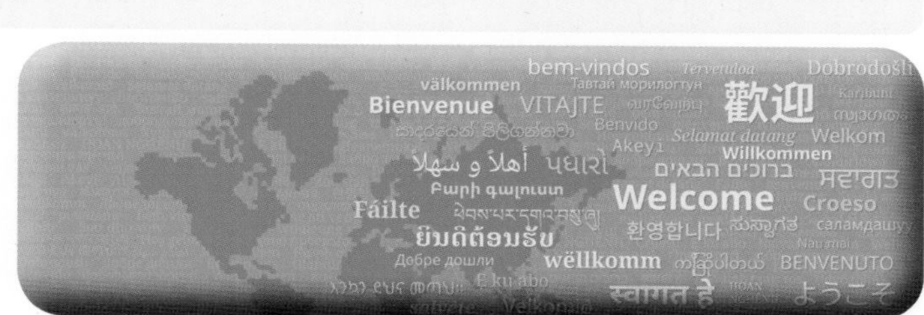

VOCA 101

belong to ~에 속하다	minority n. 소수(민족)	pass on 전달하다
generation n. 세대	at a rate of ~의 비율로	loss n. 손실, 유실
westernization n. 서구화	starvation n. 기아, 굶주림	ashamed a. 부끄러운, 수치스러운
majority n. 다수		

Review Test

정답 및 해설 p. 15

A 다음 설명에 해당하는 단어를 <보기>에서 골라 쓰시오.

〈보기〉 attempt starvation opportunity complain generation

1 ______________ suffering or death caused by lack of food

2 ______________ a chance to do something or an occasion when it is easy for you to do something

3 ______________ all people of about the same age

4 ______________ an act of trying to do something, especially something difficult

5 ______________ to say that something is wrong or not satisfactory

B 다음 밑줄 친 단어와 유사한 의미의 단어를 고르시오.

1 Nobody wants to be friends with Becky because she gossips.

① makes complaints ② tells jokes ③ spreads rumors
④ holds opinions ⑤ makes comments

2 How much water does the average person drink each day?

① outstanding ② unusual ③ abnormal
④ athletic ⑤ common

3 The rate of Korea's economic growth is likely to slow down next year.

① failure ② momentum ③ increase
④ ratio ⑤ speed

C 다음 주어진 단어를 알맞게 배열하여 우리말과 같은 뜻이 되도록 영작하시오.

1 많은 사람이 문제를 고치려고 노력하는 것보다 불평하는 게 더 쉽다는 것을 안다.
(to complain / a lot of / it / find / to fix / easier / people / try / than / them)

→ ____

2 일부 회사들은 덜 비싼 가격으로 관광객을 우주로 보낼 수 있는 우주선 개발에 착수하고 싶어 한다.
(that / creating / can take / tourists / spaceships / less expensively / some companies / into space / to start / want)

→ ____

3 이런 것들이 소수의 사회에 속한 사람들은 자신들이 언어를 다음 세대로 전파하는 것을 창피하게 생각하게 만든다. (pass on / these / people / feel ashamed / their languages / make / to / belong to / who / small communities)

→ ____

UNIT 06
1 FESTIVALS
삿포로 눈축제
2 PEOPLE
멕시코의 벽화가, 디에고 리베라
3 SOCIAL ISSUES
한국의 청소년 흡연 실태

01 FESTIVALS

1 Many winter festivals are held in countries throughout the world. ____(A)____, few of them are as impressive as the Sapporo Snow Festival in Japan. For seven days in February, the city is decorated with hundreds of beautiful snow statues and ice sculptures. Artists come together to display
5 a huge variety of sculptures. (B) These include famous buildings, people, and historical events. ⓐ They must possess a great deal of skill to design their sculptures properly. They must know how to use a variety of tools ____(C)____ chain saws and small chisels. ⓑ At night, the ice sculptures are illuminated with a dazzling display of colored lights. ⓒ The festival also
10 includes musical performances and delicious food. ⓓ There is even a beauty contest held each year. ⓔ The winner is declared the Susukino Queen of Ice. Every year about three hundred statues are created, and two million people visit Sapporo to enjoy the distinctive festival.

*chisel: 끌, (조각용) 정

영영풀이 다음 설명에 해당하는 단어를 윗글에서 찾아 넣으시오.

1 p____________ to have a particular quality or ability

2 i____________ to make a light shine on something, or to fill a place with light

3 d____________ having a special quality, character, or appearance that is different and easy to recognize

정답 및 해설 p. 15

1 윗글의 빈칸 (A)와 (C)에 들어갈 말로 가장 적절한 것은? [빈칸 완성]

(A)		(C)
① In addition	···	unlike
② However	···	such as
③ In spite of	···	such as
④ Therefore	···	as well as
⑤ In other words	···	as well as

2 What does (B) These refer to? [지칭 추론]

① tools　② artists　③ festivals　④ countries　⑤ sculptures

3 윗글의 흐름으로 보아, ⓐ ~ ⓔ 중에서 주어진 문장이 들어가기에 가장 적절한 곳은? [주어진 문장 넣기]

You can dine on seafood, potatoes, corn, and fresh dairy products.

① ⓐ　② ⓑ　③ ⓒ　④ ⓓ　⑤ ⓔ

서술형

4 삿포로 눈축제에 참여한 예술가들이 갖춰야 하는 능력을 윗글에서 찾아 우리말로 쓰시오. [세부 사항]

____

VOCA 101

throughout prep. ~의 도처에
sculpture n. 조각
performance n. 공연
impressive a. 인상적인
illuminate v. ~을 밝게 비추다
distinctive a. 눈에 띄는, 특이한
decorated with ~로 장식된
dazzling a. 눈부신, 휘황찬란한

02 PEOPLE

1 Fresco painting is a picture that is painted on a wall while the plaster is still wet. During the Renaissance in Europe, this technique was very popular, and many artists used it to decorate buildings and church vaults. 5 One of the most famous fresco painters (A) [was / were] Diego Rivera. He inspired a revival of this art form in Mexico. Born in 1886, Diego studied art in Mexico. He traveled to Europe in 1907 to continue his study of art. Once he returned to Mexico, the government agreed to (B) [sponsor / sponsoring] his work. He painted a number of murals that 10 depict scenes from Mexican history. Diego Rivera also worked in the United States. He painted murals for the City Club of the San Francisco Stock Exchange and the California School of Fine Art, and he once drew a communist picture of Lenin on the RCA Building at the Rockefeller Center in Manhattan. This created a lot of controversy for the artist, and ⓐ <u>his mural</u> was destroyed 10 shortly afterward. Even though his work was not (C) [welcomed / welcoming] by everyone, he made an impact on America's public art scene. In 1957, at the age of seventy, Rivera died in Mexico City. To this day, he is still one of Mexico's most beloved painters.

*plaster: 회반죽, 벽토(벽에 바르는 흙)

영영풀이 다음 설명에 해당하는 단어를 윗글에서 찾아 넣으시오.

1 d__________ to describe something or someone in writing or speech, or to show them in a painting, picture, etc.

2 m__________ a painting that is painted on a wall, either inside or outside a building

3 c__________ a serious argument about something that involves many people and continues for a long time

정답 및 해설 p. 16

1 What is the best title of the passage? 제목 찾기

① Rivera's Murals in Mexico
② Definition of Fresco Painting
③ Diego Rivera's Works and Life
④ People Who Draw Fresco Paintings
⑤ Diego Rivera: An Italian Renaissance Muralist

2 (A), (B), (C)의 각 괄호 안에서 어법에 맞는 표현으로 가장 적절한 것은? 어법

	(A)	(B)	(C)
①	was	··· sponsor	··· welcomed
②	was	··· sponsoring	··· welcomed
③	was	··· sponsor	··· welcoming
⑤	were	··· sponsor	··· welcoming
④	were	··· sponsoring	··· welcoming

서술형

3 밑줄 친 ⓐ his mural이 지칭하는 것을 윗글에서 찾아 영어로 쓰시오. 지칭 추론

____

VOCA 101

decorate v. 장식하다
revival n. 부흥, 부활
depict v. ~을 그리다, 묘사하다
destroy v. 파괴하다
vault n. 아치형 천장
sponsor v. ~을 후원하다
communist a. 공산주의의 n. 공산주의자
inspire v. ~에게 영감을 주다
mural n. 벽화
controversy n. 논쟁

03 SOCIAL ISSUES

Hello, everyone. I am Dr. Lee at the Ministry of Health and Welfare. Today, I want to share the result of our latest surveys of teenage smokers in Korea. We found that the number of teenage smokers has increased a lot, to a serious level. I will report the main motivation of teenagers starting smoking, why it is so serious a matter, and what should be done about this.

First, friends can have big influences over teenagers' lives. This is called "peer pressure" and this pressure can cause teenagers to start smoking. Second, teenagers begin to smoke because usually (A) <u>they</u> are curious about it. Also, students are affected by celebrities. They usually want to behave like their favorite actors or singers and when they see them smoking, teenagers think (B) <u>they</u> look cool.

Then, why is teenage cigarette smoking such a serious concern? Studies show that the earlier a teen begins smoking, the more difficult it is to break the nicotine addiction. Unfortunately, one-in-three teens who become regular smokers will die early as a result of smoking, and half of all teens who smoke will eventually die as a result of tobacco-related illnesses.

*the Ministry of Health and Welfare: 보건복지부

영영풀이 다음 설명에 해당하는 단어를 윗글에서 찾아 넣으시오.

1 m__________ the reason why you want to do something

2 c__________ wanting to know about something

3 a__________ a strong desire to do or have something regularly

정답 및 해설 p. 16

1 윗글의 밑줄 친 (A), (B)가 가리키는 것을 바르게 연결한 것은? 지칭 추론

	(A)		(B)
①	peers	…	friends
②	friends	…	students
③	teenagers	…	teenagers
④	teenagers	…	actors or singers
⑤	friends	…	actors or singers

2 윗글의 바로 뒤에 이어질 내용으로 알맞은 것은? 내용 추론

① a list of tobacco-related illnesses
② how to reduce the number of teenagers smoking
③ how many celebrities smoke in Korea
④ an interview with a teenager who smokes
⑤ how much health officials worry about teenagers smoking

3 윗글의 내용과 일치하지 않는 것은? 내용 불일치

① The number of teenagers smoking in Korea has increased.
② Some teenagers start smoking because of curiosity.
③ The earlier a teen starts smoking, the easier it is to stop smoking.
④ When friends influence your decision, it is known as peer pressure.
⑤ Half of teen smokers will die due to illnesses caused by smoking.

서술형

4 다음은 한국의 청소년 흡연에 대한 내용을 정리한 것이다. 빈칸을 채우시오. 요약문 완성하기

Korean teenagers start ______________ because they are influenced by their friends, want to be like their favorite stars, or they are just ______________. Smoking is a bad habit that has no benefits.

VOCA 101

survey n. 조사
behave v. 행동하다
tobacco-related a. 담배와 연관된
motivation n. 자극, 동기
concern n. 걱정, 근심
peer n. 동료, 또래
addiction n. 중독

정답 및 해설 p. 17

A 다음 설명에 해당하는 단어를 <보기>에서 골라 쓰시오.

〈보기〉	controversy	distinctive	addiction	motivation	possess

1 ______________ a strong desire to do or have something regularly

2 ______________ a serious argument about something that involves many people and continues for a long time

3 ______________ the reason why you want to do something

4 ______________ having a special quality, character, or appearance that is different and easy to recognize

5 ______________ to have a particular quality or ability

B 다음 밑줄 친 단어와 유사한 의미의 단어를 고르시오.

1 The National Museum will display the works of some modern artists.
① picture ② fix ③ attend
④ reserve ⑤ exhibit

2 Her lecture really inspired us to protect the environment.
① insisted ② stimulated ② discouraged
④ taught ⑤ erupted

3 Some of the adult fans behaved like kids at the ball park.
① performed ② functioned ② carried out
④ acted ⑤ applied

C 다음 주어진 단어를 알맞게 배열하여 우리말과 같은 뜻이 되도록 영작하시오.

1 그들은 전기톱과 작은 끌 같은 다양한 도구를 사용하는 방법을 알아야 한다. (chain saws / how to use / a variety of / they / such as / tools / must / and / small chisels / know)

→ ____

2 그는 멕시코 역사를 묘사하는 수많은 벽화를 그렸다. (painted / depict / a number of / he / that / Mexican history / murals / from / scenes)

→ ____

3 십 대가 흡연을 일찍 시작할수록 니코틴 중독에서 벗어나는 것은 더욱 어렵다. (a teen / it is / the earlier / the nicotine addiction / to break / smoking / the more difficult / begins)

→ ____

UNIT 07
1 HISTORY
농민을 위한 프랑스혁명
2 ANIMALS
매머드를 본 적이 있나요?
3 ENVIRONMENT
하늘에 뚫린 구멍

The French Revolution, which began in 1789 and lasted for about ten years, was an important event in Western history. Ultimately, the revolution caused the downfall of the monarchy's power in France. Several factors contributed to the French Revolution. Prior to the revolution, the quality of life in Europe had been determined by family status. If you were born into a poor family, your life would be one of poverty. ⓐ It was not possible to raise your status if you were poor. Unfair tax laws left the poor without much money. Severe food shortages also caused a lot of hardship for the peasants. On the other hand, the wealthy enjoyed a life of comfort, and the monarchy did not seem to care about the fate of the peasantry. The peasantry became terribly resentful of the wealthy aristocracy. They wanted greater equality in French society, and in 1789 they finally launched a violent political revolution which changed France's political landscape and gave political power to the people of France.

영영풀이 다음 설명에 해당하는 단어를 윗글에서 찾아 넣으시오.

1 r__________ a time when people change a ruler or political system by using force or violence

2 s__________ a situation in which there is not enough of something that people need

3 r__________ feeling angry and upset about something that you think is unfair

정답 및 해설 p. 18

1 윗글의 제목으로 가장 적절한 것은? [제목 찾기]

① How to Raise Your Status in France
② Causes and Effects of the French Revolution
③ Reasons for the French Revolution's Failure
④ The Life of the French Peasantry in the Countryside
⑤ The French Revolution's Effect on Western History

2 윗글의 밑줄 친 ⓐ It과 쓰임이 같은 것은? [어법]

① It was so boring that I fell asleep.
② It is not mine, but you can use it.
③ It was Henry that took that beautiful picture.
④ It is difficult to translate Korean into English.
⑤ It is still raining outside, so I'd rather stay home.

3 윗글에서 프랑스혁명의 발발 원인으로 언급된 것이 아닌 것은? [내용 불일치]

① 가난의 대물림
② 불공평한 세금
③ 식량의 부족
④ 부유한 귀족 계급을 향한 분노
⑤ 왕의 폭력적인 군림

VOCA 101

revolution n. 혁명
factor n. 요인
determine v. ~을 결정하다
hardship n. 시련, 고난
resentful a. 분개한
launch v. ~을 일으키다
downfall n. 몰락
prior to ~ 전에
poverty n. 가난
peasant n. 소작농
aristocracy n. 귀족
monarchy n. 군주 정치, 군주 일가
status n. 지위, 신분
shortage n. 부족
peasantry n. 소작농들
equality n. 평등

02 ANIMALS

Have you ever come face-to-face with a giant wooly mammoth? If you have, then it must have been inside a museum because this magnificent beast is now extinct. The wooly mammoth was one of the largest creatures that had ever inhabited the Earth. It often grew to be sixteen-feet tall and weighed between six and eight tons. Why don't these animals roam the Earth now? About 10,000 years ago, the number of wooly mammoths started to decline, and by around 1,600 B.C., the few remaining specimens of this species died out. ⓐ Many researchers have concluded that climate change was a significant factor. ⓑ 12,000 years ago, the Earth's climate began to heat up, so icy regions of land around the world began to melt. ⓒ This phenomenon is called "glacial retreat," and it drastically reduced the wooly mammoth's natural habitat. ⓓ The spread of advanced human hunters was likely a major cause of the mammoth's extinction. ⓔ In fact, scientists have discovered cave drawings that illustrate ______(A)______.

*wooly mammoth: 털매머드

영영풀이 다음 설명에 해당하는 단어를 윗글에서 찾아 넣으시오.

1 r________ to walk or travel, usually for a long time, with no clear purpose or direction
2 s________ a single example of something, often an animal or plant
3 d________ extremely and suddenly

1 What is the best title of the passage? 제목 찾기

① The Animals You Can See in a Museum
② The Reason Why Glacial Retreat Took Place
③ The Place Where You Can Find a Wooly Mammoth
④ Research on the Wooly Mammoth's Natural Habitat
⑤ Reasons Why the Wooly Mammoth Disappeared

2 윗글의 흐름으로 보아, ⓐ ~ ⓔ 중에서 주어진 문장이 들어가기에 가장 적절한 곳은? 주어진 문장 넣기

Another factor that contributed to the extinction of the wooly mammoth was human activity.

① ⓐ ② ⓑ ③ ⓒ ④ ⓓ ⑤ ⓔ

3 윗글의 빈칸 (A)에 들어갈 말로 가장 적절한 것은? 빈칸 완성

① people raising wooly mammoths
② humans hunting wooly mammoths
③ wooly mammoths living on glaciers
④ the natural habitat of wooly mammoths
⑤ some kids playing with wooly mammoths

4 윗글에서 다음 설명에 해당하는 단어를 찾아 영어로 쓰시오. (1단어) 어휘

the place where a particular animal or plant usually lives in or a particular plant usually grows in

____

VOCA 101

magnificent a. 장엄한
inhabit v. 살다
specimen n. 표본, 실례
drastically ad. 급격하게
extinct a. 멸종의
roam v. ~을 돌아다니다
glacial a. 빙하의
creature n. 생물, 피조물
decline v. 감소하다
retreat n. 후퇴

03 ENVIRONMENT

1 The first hole in the ozone layer was found in 1984. (A) Scientists discovered that the amount of ozone above Antarctica was much less than normal. Since then other ozone holes were found over other parts of the world. Why does it matter?

5 The ozone layer is important because it protects us from the ultraviolet light that comes from the sun. (B) This ultraviolet light called UV-B, is bad for people, animals, and plants. (C) It's important to use sun block creams every day. It can cause cancers, hurt animals' eyes and also reduce the growth rate of some plants.

10 The holes in the ozone layer are caused by certain gases we release. These gases are called CFCs (chlorofluorocarbons). (D) They are found in refrigerators, in car air conditioning systems, aerosols, etc. Other gases called halons that are used in fire extinguishers also make holes in the ozone layer. (E) The only possible solution to the problem is using and making less products that contain

15 CFCs or halons.

*chlorofluorocarbon: 염화불화탄소 **halon: 할론

영영풀이 다음 설명에 해당하는 단어를 윗글에서 찾아 넣으시오.

1 r__________ to make something smaller or less in size, amount, or price

2 r__________ the number of times something happens, or the number of examples of something within a certain period

3 r__________ to let a substance flow out

정답 및 해설 p. 19

1 윗글의 주제로 알맞은 것은? 주제 찾기

① the holes in the ozone layer
② the ozone layer
③ ultraviolet light
④ CFCs
⑤ halons

2 윗글의 밑줄 친 (A) ~ (E) 중, 전체 흐름과 관계가 <u>없는</u> 것은? 무관한 문장 찾기

① (A) ② (B) ③ (C) ④ (D) ⑤ (E)

3 윗글의 내용으로 볼 때, 오존층이 중요한 이유는? 세부 사항

① It protects us from halons.
② It protects us from the UV light.
③ It protects us from CFCs.
④ It causes global warming.
⑤ It lets us use refrigerators and car air conditioning systems.

4 다음은 윗글의 내용을 요약한 것이다. 빈칸을 채우시오. 요약문 완성하기

_________________ is very important for our environment, but since 1984, several ozone holes were found all over the world. This can cause serious problems for people, animals, and plants. Scientists say that the only way to protect the ozone layer is using and making fewer products that contain harmful gases, like __________ or __________.

VOCA 101

ozone layer n. 오존층
ultraviolet a. 자외선의
release v. 배출하다, 내놓다
solution n. 해결책
Antarctica n. 남극대륙
sun block cream n. 자외선 차단 크림
aerosol n. 에어로졸, 연무기
normal a. 표준의, 평범한
growth rate n. 성장률
fire extinguisher n. 소화기

정답 및 해설 p. 20

A 다음 설명에 해당하는 단어를 <보기>에서 골라 쓰시오.

〈보기〉	revolution	drastically	resentful	roam	reduce

1 ______________ extremely and suddenly

2 ______________ a time when people change a ruler or political system by using force or violence

3 ______________ to make something smaller or less in size, amount, or price

4 ______________ to walk or travel, usually for a long time, with no clear purpose or direction

5 ______________ feeling angry and upset about something that you think is unfair

B 다음 밑줄 친 단어와 유사한 의미의 단어를 고르시오.

1 I think that the unfair distribution of wealth is the most serious problem.

① unjust ② indifferent ③ expensive
④ inaccurate ⑤ even

2 Many wild animals inhabit this forest. We shouldn't develop the forest.

① inherit ② inhibit ③ dwell in
④ migrate ⑤ hide

3 Please don't breathe in the gas released during the chemical reaction.

① collected ② emitted ③ vanished
④ obtained ⑤ published

C 다음 주어진 단어를 알맞게 배열하여 우리말과 같은 뜻이 되도록 영작하시오.

1 군주 일가는 소작농들의 운명에는 관심이 없어 보였다. (seem to / the fate / the monarchy / did not / the peasantry / of / care about)

→ ____

2 털매머드의 멸종에 기여한 또 다른 요소는 인간의 활동이었다. (the wooly mammoth / factor / the extinction / was / another / contributed to / human activity / that / of)

→ ____

3 오존층의 구멍은 우리가 방출하는 어떤 기체 때문에 생긴다. (are / we / the holes / in the ozone layer / certain / caused / gases / release / by)

→ ____

UNIT 08
1 ART
예술은 벗어남이다, 인상주의
2 SPECIAL DAYS
가장 값싸게 쇼핑하는 날, 박싱데이
3 SPACE
화성에서 살 수 있을까?

01 ART

Impressionist artwork originated in France during the nineteenth century. Impressionism was a significant departure from traditional artwork. Before Impressionism, artwork usually (A) [depicted / was depicted] royalty or religious figures, who were usually placed in the center of the painting. However, the background of the painting was not important. The introduction of Impressionism changed the old belief of what art was and how artwork was created. Artists began to focus on illustrating beautiful outdoor scenes. Impressionist artists often painted landscapes, people, and historical events. They used not only direct but reflected light to depict nature objectively. This was very different from (B)[that / what] most people were accustomed to seeing. Every part of the painting was important. Furthermore, the people that were depicted in the paintings were not always from a royal family. ________________ The subject of a painting could be a person (C) [walked / walking] in a park, or it could be a bartender in a tavern. Some famous impressionist painters include Renoir, Monet, and Degas.

*Impressionist: a. 인상주의의 n. 인상파 화가

영영풀이 다음 설명에 해당하는 단어를 윗글에서 찾아 넣으시오.

1 d________ a way of doing something that is different from the usual, traditional, or expected way

2 f________ someone who is important or famous in some way

3 a________ familiar with something

정답 및 해설 p. 21

1 (A), (B), (C)의 각 괄호 안에서 어법에 맞는 표현으로 가장 적절한 것은? 어법

	(A)		(B)		(c)
①	depicted	…	what	…	walking
②	was depicted	…	what	…	walking
③	was depicted	…	that	…	walked
④	was depicted	…	that	…	walking
⑤	depicted	…	what	…	walked

2 윗글의 빈칸에 들어갈 말로 가장 적절한 것은? 빈칸 완성

① Anybody could paint!
② Nobody could paint!
③ Nobody could be painted!
④ Anybody could be painted!
⑤ Nobody could buy paintings!

3 윗글의 내용과 일치하지 <u>않는</u> 것은? 내용 불일치

① 인상주의는 19세기 프랑스에서 시작되었다.
② 인상주의 시대 이전의 그림은 배경을 중시했다.
③ 인상주의 시대의 그림은 자연을 객관적으로 묘사했다.
④ 인상주의 시대 그림의 소재는 이전 시대의 그림보다 다양했다.
⑤ 르누아르(Renoir)와 모네(Monet)는 인상주의 화가이다.

4 윗글에서 알맞은 표현을 찾아 주어진 문장을 영작하시오. (7단어) 문장 완성

나는 일찍 일어나는 것에 익숙했다. (get up)

____

VOCA 101

originate v. 비롯되다, 유래하다
figure n. 인물
accustomed a. 익숙해진
departure n. 이탈, 벗어남; 출발
landscape n. 경치, 풍경
subject n. 주제
royalty n. 왕족
objectively ad. 객관적으로
tavern n. 술집

02 SPECIAL DAYS

Boxing Day is one of the best shopping days of the year. It takes place on December 26, just after Christmas. For many stores, Boxing Day generates the highest revenues of the year. They often sell their products at highly discounted prices. This attracts huge crowds of people. Stores are always full of shoppers on Boxing Day. Sometimes, people even wait outside of stores before they open. ⓐ They have a good chance to get products at the lowest prices. ⓑ They hope to purchase cheap televisions, clothes, or furniture. ⓒ Once inside, they often rush around and grab whatever they can. ⓓ They even get into fights over merchandise! ⓔ Boxing Day sales have the potential to create customer stampedes, injuries, and even fatalities. In order to protect customers, they often limit the number of people who are allowed inside.

*stampede: 몰려들기, 쇄도

영영풀이 다음 설명에 해당하는 단어를 윗글에서 찾아 넣으시오.

1 g__________ to produce or cause something

2 p__________ the possibility that something will develop in a particular way, or have a particular effect

3 f__________ a death in an accident or a violent attack

정답 및 해설 p. 21

1 윗글의 제목으로 가장 적절한 것은? 제목 찾기

① The Origins of Boxing Day
② A Place to Buy Cheap Products
③ Particular Aspects of Boxing Day
④ How to Get the Highest Revenues
⑤ Relationship Between Christmas and Boxing Day

2 윗글의 흐름으로 보아, ⓐ ~ ⓔ 중에서 주어진 문장이 들어가기에 가장 적절한 곳은? 주어진 문장 넣기

However, Boxing Day can also make people a little bit crazy.

① ⓐ ② ⓑ ③ ⓒ ④ ⓓ ⑤ ⓔ

3 윗글을 읽고, 빈칸 (A)와 (B)에 들어갈 말로 가장 적절한 것을 고르시오. 세부 사항

People think that companies sell their products at ___(A)___ price on Boxing Day, so the shops usually have ___(B)___ customers of the year.

	(A)		(B)
①	half	…	the best
②	the best	…	the most
③	the lowest	…	the least
④	the highest	…	the most
⑤	the most reasonable	…	the least

서술형

4 윗글에서 박싱데이에 상점에 들어오는 손님의 수를 제한하는 이유를 찾아 우리말로 쓰시오. 세부 사항

____

VOCA 101

generate v. 산출하다	revenue n. 수익	product n. 제품, 상품
purchase v. ~을 구입하다	rush v. 급하게 가다, 돌진하다	merchandise n. 상품
potential n. 잠재성, 가능성	fatality n. 죽음	limit v. 제한하다

03 SPACE

Nowadays there are lots of disease, pollution, and war on Earth so people think that humans might live on another planet sometime. Most planets are hotter than the places on the Earth's equator, colder than the Earth's north or south poles, or too far away for people to live.

However, many scientists think that Mars might be a planet where people could live in the future. It would take a long time to travel to Mars, but it is still the closest planet to Earth. A short time ago the United States sent a spacecraft to Mars ________________. Now it is proven that there is water on Mars. If there is water, then it might be possible for humans to live there. This is important because all humans need water to live, and also, the water could be used to make fuel to return back to Earth. However, Mars can have too much wind and not enough oxygen, which might make it difficult for people to live there. Would you like to go there sometime soon?

영영풀이 다음 설명에 해당하는 단어를 윗글에서 찾아 넣으시오.

1 p________________ damage caused to water, air, etc. by harmful substances or waste

2 p________________ to show that something is true by providing facts, information, etc.

3 f________________ a substance such as coal, gas, or oil that can be burned to produce heat or energy

정답 및 해설 p. 22

1 윗글의 목적으로 가장 알맞은 것은? 목적 찾기

① to compare Earth and Mars
② to warn people about environmental pollution
③ to report why we can't live on Earth anymore
④ to explain about possibility of living on Mars in the future
⑤ to persuade readers that they should visit Mars as soon as possible

2 윗글의 빈칸에 들어갈 내용으로 가장 알맞은 것은? 빈칸 완성

① without anyone knowing
② to search for water
③ to check its temperature
④ for the first time and lost communication with it
⑤ to find out whether there is any living creature

3 윗글에서 화성에 대해 글쓴이가 직접적으로 언급하지 않은 것은? 내용 불일치

① Mars is the closest planet to Earth.
② Mars has too much wind.
③ There is water on Mars.
④ Mars is much colder than Earth.
⑤ Mars doesn't have enough oxygen.

4 다음은 윗글의 내용을 요약한 것이다. 빈칸을 채우시오. 요약문 완성하기

There are lots of problems on __________. People might leave Earth and live on another planet. However, most planets are too hot, cold or far away for people to visit. __________ is the closest planet to Earth. It has water and humans might be able to live there.

disease n. 질병	pollution n. 오염	equator n. 적도
prove v. 증명하다	fuel n. 연료	oxygen n. 산소

정답 및 해설 p. 23

A 다음 설명에 해당하는 단어를 <보기>에서 골라 쓰시오.

〈보기〉 accustomed pollution figure fuel generate

1 ______________ damage caused to water, air, etc. by harmful substances or waste

2 ______________ someone who is important or famous in some way

3 ______________ a substance such as coal, gas, or oil that can be burned to produce heat or energy

4 ______________ to produce or cause something

5 ______________ familiar with something

B 다음 밑줄 친 단어와 유사한 의미의 단어를 고르시오.

1 The earliest glassware originated in ancient Egypt.

① ordered ② terminated ③ started
④ resulted ⑤ located

2 You can find expensive products from Europe on the 2nd floor.

① clothing ② goods ③ customers
④ manufacturers ⑤ factories

3 It is not yet proven that this new medicine is effective.

① suggested ② compared ③ warned
④ demonstrated ⑤ protected

C 다음 주어진 단어를 알맞게 배열하여 우리말과 같은 뜻이 되도록 영작하시오.

1 그들은 자연을 객관적으로 묘사하기 위해 직사광선뿐 아니라 반사광선도 사용했다.
(depict / not only / but / they / nature / reflected light / direct / objectively / to / used)

→ ____

2 그들은 일단 상점에 발을 들여놓으면 마구 돌아다니면서 닥치는 대로 물건을 집는다.
(whatever / once / grab / rush around / they / they / inside / can / and / often)

→ ____

3 많은 과학자들이 화성은 사람들이 미래에 살 수 있는 행성일지도 모른다고 생각한다. (where / Mars / in the future / a planet / many scientists / could live / people / that / think / might be)

→ ____

UNIT 09
1 PLACES
영국과 프랑스를 터널로 연결하다
2 TRAGEDY
팝의 제왕의 죽음
3 WORLD NEWS
속세를 등진 사람들, 아미시

01 PLACES

1 **The Channel Tunnel** is one of the most amazing feats of engineering in the world. Known as "The Chunnel," it operates between Great Britain and France. The tunnel is built underneath the English Channel. In fact, it is the longest undersea tunnel in the world. It was designed to make travel from Europe to
5 the British Isles easier. ⓐ The idea for an underwater tunnel between England and France was initially suggested in 1802. ⓑ Finally, the Chunnel officially opened in 1994. ⓒ There have been (A) <u>some problems</u> in the underground tunnel since it opened. ⓓ Several small fires have stopped service in the tunnel. ⓔ Initially, there was also a problem with illegal immigrants entering
10 Britain. However, both of these issues have been examined thoroughly, and the emergency staff in the tunnel are well-trained to handle any situations.

*the English Channel: 영국 해협 (영국과 프랑스 사이에 있는 해협)

영영풀이 다음 설명에 해당하는 단어를 윗글에서 찾아 넣으시오.

1 f________ something that is an impressive achievement, because it needs a lot of skill, strength, etc. to do
2 i________ at the beginning
3 t________ carefully, so that nothing is forgotten

정답 및 해설 p. 24

1 윗글을 통해서 알 수 있는 것은? 세부 내용

① The English suggested the idea of the underwater tunnel.
② Initially, the purpose of the Chunnel was to carry goods.
③ It took about a century to build the Chunnel.
④ There still exists the problem of illegal immigrants.
⑤ There are emergency staff in the tunnel to deal with problems.

2 윗글의 흐름으로 보아, ⓐ ~ ⓔ 중에서 다음 문장이 들어가기에 가장 적절한 곳은? 주어진 문장 넣기

However, it was only in the 1980s that construction began on the project.

① ⓐ ② ⓑ ③ ⓒ ④ ⓓ ⑤ ⓔ

서술형

3 윗글에서 밑줄 친 (A) some problems에 해당하는 것을 찾아 우리말로 쓰시오. 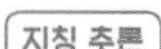 지칭 추론

____

VOCA 101

feat n. 위업
underneath prep. ~의 아래에
immigrant n. 이민[이주]자
emergency n. 비상 상황
engineering n. 공학기술
officially ad. 공식적으로
examine v. 조사하다
handle v. 다루다, 처리하다
operate v. 움직이다
initially ad. 처음에
thoroughly ad. 철저히

02 TRAGEDY

Who is the King of Pop? It's Michael Jackson! He revolutionized music through music videos, song writing, and live performances. Michael Jackson's musical career started ① at a very early age.

(A)

However, on June 25, 2009, news of the pop star's death shocked the world. He ⓐ [has suffered from / had suffered from] a cardiac arrest. Michael was taking several different medications at the time of his death. They included several types of painkillers. Doctors said that misuse of medication administered by his personal physician played a role ② in his untimely death.

(B)

He was only eight years old when he became the lead singer of the Jackson 5. The Jackson 5 ⓑ [consisted of / was consisted of] Michael and his brothers. Eventually, Michael began a solo career, and in the early 1980s he became the King of Pop. He wrote some of the most popular music ③ of all time. Songs such as *Billie Jean* and *Thriller* helped to make him a musical superstar.

(C)

④ Millions of fans around the world showed their love and support. They built memorials ⑤ in honor of Michael and sang his songs together. His memory will live on through his unforgettable music.

*cardiac arrest: 심장 마비

영영풀이 다음 설명에 해당하는 단어를 윗글에서 찾아 넣으시오.

1 l__________ given or made when people are watching, not recorded
2 s__________ to have a particular disease or medical condition
3 a__________ to give someone a medicine or medical treatment

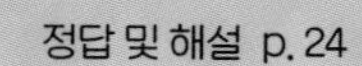
정답 및 해설 p. 24

1 윗글 (A), (B), (C)의 순서로 가장 적절한 것은? [글의 순서 정하기]

① (A) – (C) – (B)　② (B) – (A) – (C)　③ (B) – (C) – (A)
④ (C) – (A) – (B)　⑤ (C) – (B) – (A)

2 ⓐ와 ⓑ의 각 괄호 안에서 어법에 맞는 표현으로 가장 적절한 것을 골라 쓰시오. [어법]

ⓐ ____________________　ⓑ ____________________

3 윗글의 밑줄 친 ① ~ ⑤ 중, 해석이 바르게 되지 <u>않은</u> 것은? [의미 파악]

① 아주 어린 나이에　② 그의 때 이른 죽음에　③ 전 시대를 통틀어서
④ 백만 명의 팬들이　⑤ 마이클을 기리기 위해

서술형

4 According to the doctors, what was the cause of Michael Jackson's death? (8단어) 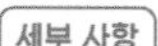 [세부 사항]

____

VOCA 101

revolutionize v. ~을 대변혁하다	suffer v. 고통받다	medication n. 약물
painkiller n. 진통제	misuse n. 오용, 남용	administer v. (약물을) 투여하다
physician n. 내과의사	untimely a. 때 아닌, 때 이른	memorial n. 기념물

03 WORLD NEWS

1 Who are the Amish? (A) The Amish population is about 140,000 and they live in places like Lancaster County, Pennsylvania and Ontario, Canada. The Amish are famous for rejecting modern culture and keeping their lifestyle tied into their religion. They believe literally everything written in the Bible. They
5 believe that they should keep themselves away from the larger society.
(B) Amish men wear black suits, black shoes and straw broad-brimmed hats. Amish women wear solid-colored dresses with a cape and apron. (C) Many Amish couples have seven or eight children. Amish children go to school until they finish the eighth grade. Amish people don't think the modern technology
10 helps to improve human lives.
(D) Lately, many tourists visit Amish communities and observe their singular way of living. (E)

영영풀이 다음 설명에 해당하는 단어를 윗글에서 찾아 넣으시오.

1 i__________ to make something better, or to become better
2 o__________ to see and notice something
3 d__________ to be different from something or someone

정답 및 해설 p. 25

1 윗글의 빈칸 (A)~(E) 중, 다음 문장이 들어가기에 가장 알맞은 곳은? 주어진 문장 넣기

Their lifestyle differs from other modern people's.

① (A) ② (B) ③ (C) ④ (D) ⑤ (E)

2 윗글을 통해 알 수 있는 아미시 사람들의 성품으로 알맞은 것은? 내용 이해

① pious
② worldly
③ selfish
④ civilized
⑤ pessimistic

3 윗글의 내용으로 볼 때, 아미시 사람들의 생활 방식이라고 짐작되지 않는 것은? 내용 불일치

① They like to live in the country away from cities.
② Women wear solid-colored dresses.
③ Men wear black shoes.
④ Children don't go to school after eighth grade.
⑤ They learn some foreign languages to communicate with tourists.

서술형

4 다음은 아미시 사람들의 생활 방식을 정리한 것이다. 빈칸을 채우시오. 요약문 완성하기

The Amish are people who live differently from others rejecting __________ culture. They believe everything written in the __________, and think they should keep themselves away from the larger society. Because of their unique lifestyle, many tourists visit their __________ and observe their singular way of living.

VOCA 101

lifestyle n. 생활 방식
broad-brimmed a. 테가 넓은
improve v. 개선하다, 향상시키다
differ from ~와 다르다
literally ad. 문자 그대로
solid a. 짙은
singular a. 특이한, 별개의
the Bible n. 성경
cape n. 망토
way of living n. 생활 방식

정답 및 해설 p. 26

A 다음 설명에 해당하는 단어를 <보기>에서 골라 쓰시오.

〈보기〉 improve live suffer thoroughly feat

1 ______________ given or made when people are watching, not recorded

2 ______________ to have a particular disease or medical condition

3 ______________ something that is an impressive achievement, because it needs a lot of skill, strength, etc. to do

4 ______________ carefully, so that nothing is forgotten

5 ______________ to make something better, or to become better

B 다음 밑줄 친 단어와 유사한 의미의 단어를 고르시오.

1 I can handle these problems by myself, so you don't have to worry.

① take over ② hold ③ charge
④ carry ⑤ deal with

2 Everybody was shocked by his untimely death.

① accidental ② later ③ recent
④ early ⑤ uncertainly

3 The lucky visitors could observe the whale giving birth to a calf in the aquarium.

① record ② remember ③ join
④ praise ⑤ watch

C 다음 주어진 단어를 알맞게 배열하여 우리말과 같은 뜻이 되도록 영작하시오.

1 그 프로젝트에 대한 공사가 추진되기 시작한 것은 겨우 1980년대가 되어서였다.
(that / on the project / was / in the 1980s / construction / it / began / only)

→ ____

2 그는 잭슨 파이브의 리드 싱어가 되었을 때 겨우 여덟 살이었다. (the lead singer / only / was / when / eight years old / became / he / he / of the Jackson 5)

→ ____

3 아미시인들은 현대 문화를 거부하고, 자신의 생활양식을 종교에 귀착시켜 생활하는 것으로 유명하다.
(modern culture / keeping / the Amish / into their religion / famous for / and / rejecting / their lifestyle / are / tied)

→ ____

UNIT 10
1 CAMPAIGN
어떻게 하면 북극곰을 보호할 수 있을까?
2 FUTURE LIFE
식품은 어떻게 변화하는가?
3 HISTORY
알래스카, 머나먼 미국의 땅

01 CAMPAIGN

1 Did you know that February 27 is International Polar Bear Day? Polar bears were the first species to become endangered (A) [because of / because] climate change. 기후가 따뜻해지면 질수록, 북극의 얼음이 더 많이 녹게 될 것이다. ⓐ This poses a significant threat to the polar bear's home and its survival. ⓑ If you want to help protect
5 the polar bear, there are numerous ways for you to contribute. There (B) [are / is] currently several organizations dedicated to saving the polar bear. ⓒ They include the National Wildlife Federation and Polar Bears International. ⓓ Polar bears are carnivorous, mostly eating seals. Each monetary donation to these organizations (C) [will put / will be put] toward helping save polar bears.
10 ⓔ You can also help by making an effort to conserve energy and by using public transportation to reduce your carbon footprint. Slowing global warming will help to preserve the polar bear's natural habitat. Even the smallest changes can make a huge difference!

*carbon footprint: 탄소 발자국 (이산화탄소의 배출량)
**National Wildlife Federation: 미국야생동식물연맹

영영풀이 다음 설명에 해당하는 단어를 윗글에서 찾아 넣으시오.

1 d________ something, especially money, that you give to a person or an organization in order to help them
2 p________ to save something or someone from being harmed or destroyed
3 h________ the natural home of a plant or animal

1 윗글의 제목으로 가장 적절한 것은? 제목 찾기

① What Polar Bears Eat
② Where Polar Bears Live
③ How to Help Polar Bears
④ International Polar Bear Day
⑤ How to Reduce Your Carbon Footprint

2 (A), (B), (C)의 각 괄호 안에서 어법에 맞는 표현으로 가장 적절한 것은? 어법

	(A)		(B)		(C)
①	because of	…	are	…	will be put
②	because of	…	are	…	will put
③	because of	…	is	…	will put
④	because	…	are	…	will put
⑤	because	…	is	…	will be put

서술형

3 윗글의 밑줄 친 우리말과 같은 뜻이 되도록 문장을 완성하시오. 문장 완성

____________________ (warm) the climate gets, ____________________ (much) the ice in the Arctic will melt.

4 윗글의 ⓐ ~ ⓔ 중, 글의 흐름과 관계없는 문장은? 무관한 문장 찾기

① ⓐ ② ⓑ ③ ⓒ ④ ⓓ ⑤ ⓔ

VOCA 101

endangered a. 멸종 위기의
numerous a. 매우 많은
dedicated to ~에 전념하는
effort n. 노력
habitat n. 서식지
significant a. 상당한
carnivorous a. 육식성의
monetary a. 재정적인
conserve v. 아끼다, 보호하다
pose a threat to ~에게 위협을 가하다
organization n. 기구, 단체
donation n. 기부금
preserve v. ~을 지키다, 보존하다

02 FUTURE LIFE

1 Scientists have the ability to achieve some truly amazing things nowadays. Did you know that they can genetically modify our food? It's true. In the past, farmers have used traditional breeding techniques to grow their crops. 5 ① They would do this by harvesting seeds from their best crops. Then, ② they would plant those seeds the next year. This method, which is used to improve the quality and the quantity of crops, is called hybridization. Even though ③ they come from their best crops, this method of breeding had many limits. ⓐ Scientists have found ways to 10 break those limits. They can modify crops to make them ______(A)______ bacteria, viruses, and pests. ⓑ This helps to reduce the quantity of pesticides farmers use to protect ④ their crops. In addition, modifying seeds can help ⑤ them produce ______(B)______ crops. ⓒ For instance, nobody knows how safe genetically modified food really is. ⓓ There have not been any experiments 15 designed to test the long-term effects of genetically modified food. ⓔ

*hybridization: 이종 교배(다른 종(種) 간의 교배)

영영풀이 다음 설명에 해당하는 단어를 윗글에서 찾아 넣으시오.

1 m______________ to make small changes to something in order to improve it and make it more suitable or effective

2 b______________ to keep animals or plants in order to produce babies or new plants, especially ones with particular qualities

3 m______________ a planned way of doing something, especially one that a lot of people know about and use

정답 및 해설 p. 27

1 윗글의 밑줄 친 ① ~ ⑤가 가리키는 대상이 나머지 넷과 다른 것은? [지칭 추론]

① ② ③ ④ ⑤

2 윗글의 빈칸 (A)와 (B)에 들어갈 말로 가장 적절한 것은? [빈칸 완성]

	(A)		(B)
①	more vulnerable to	…	the best
②	more receptive to	…	stranger
③	less immune to	…	some unknown
④	more resistant to	…	a larger quantity of
⑤	less fragile to	…	a smaller quantity of

3 윗글의 흐름으로 보아, ⓐ ~ ⓔ 중에서 주어진 문장이 들어가기에 가장 적절한 곳은? [주어진 문장 넣기]

However, there is also a downside.

① ⓐ ② ⓑ ③ ⓒ ④ ⓓ ⑤ ⓔ

4 윗글에서 유전자 변형 식품(genetically modified food)의 안전성을 믿을 수 없는 이유를 찾아 우리말로 쓰시오. [이유 찾기]

VOCA 101

achieve v. 이루다
traditional a. 전통적인
quality n. 질
design v. 고안하다
genetically ad. 유전적으로
breed v. 번식시키다, 품종 개량을 하다
quantity n. 양
downside n. 불리한 면, 단점
modify v. ~을 변경[변형]하다
seed n. 씨, 종자
pesticide n. 살충제

03 HISTORY

U.S. bought Alaska from Russia for 7 million dollars in 1867. Most Americans thought it was a big mistake and waste of money. They called Alaska "Seward's Folly" or "Seward's Icebox." They named it after William H. Seward, the Secretary of State of the United States, who insisted the purchase. However, gold was discovered between 1896 and 1902, and whole cities grew almost overnight. By then, many Alaskans fought for the statehood, but the government ignored them. During World War II, in 1941, America declared war on Japan, and Alaska's strategic position became very important. The U.S. government began to seriously consider its statehood. Alaskans elected delegates, who met President Eisenhower. They convinced him to sign the Alaska Statehood Act in 1958. Finally, on January 3, 1959 Alaska became the forty-ninth state of the United States of America.

영영풀이 다음 설명에 해당하는 단어를 윗글에서 찾아 넣으시오.

1 i__________ to demand that something happen or that somebody agree to do something

2 i__________ to intentionally not listen or give attention to

3 c__________ to persuade someone or make someone certain

정답 및 해설 p. 28

1 윗글의 주제로 알맞은 것은? [주제 찾기]

① Alaska becoming the 49th U.S. state
② the purchase of Alaska
③ the discovery of gold in Alaska
④ the economy and people of Alaska
⑤ a meeting with President Eisenhower

2 윗글을 읽고 추론할 수 있는 것은? [내용 추론]

① Eisenhower was born in Alaska when it was a Russian state.
② Eisenhower always wanted to sign the Alaska Statehood Act.
③ Eisenhower resigned before the Alaska Statehood Act.
④ Eisenhower was considering signing the Statehood Act before meeting the delegates.
⑤ Eisenhower tried to invade Japan with the Russian military during World War II.

3 윗글을 읽고 미국인들이 알래스카를 밑줄 친 **Seward's Folly**와 같이 부른 이유를 영어로 쓰시오. [이유 찾기]

____

____

4 다음은 알래스카가 미국의 49번째 주가 되기까지의 과정을 정리한 것이다. 빈칸을 채우시오. [요약문 완성하기]

The United States bought Alaska from ______________ in 1867. Some years later ______________ was discovered in Alaska and during World War II, it became an important spot for strategic purposes. With these reasons, the U.S. government decided to make it the forty-ninth state. Finally, President Eisenhower signed ______________ in 1958, and Alaska became ______________ of the United States in 1959.

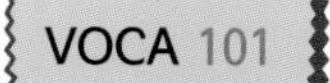

VOCA 101

name after ~의 이름을 따서 짓다
ignore v. 무시하다
delegate n. 대표, 사절
insist v. 주장하다
strategic a. 전략적인
convince v. 확신시키다, 설득하다
statehood n. 주(州)로서의 지위
elect v. 뽑다, 선출하다
act n. 법령

Review Test

정답 및 해설 p. 29

A 다음 설명에 해당하는 단어를 <보기>에서 골라 쓰시오.

〈보기〉 convince modify method donation ignore

1 ______________ something, especially money, that you give to a person or an organization in order to help them

2 ______________ to intentionally not listen or give attention to

3 ______________ to make small changes to something in order to improve it and make it more suitable or effective

4 ______________ a planned way of doing something, especially one that a lot of people know about and use

5 ______________ to persuade someone or make someone certain

B 다음 밑줄 친 단어와 유사한 의미의 단어를 고르시오.

1 We should conserve the rainforests for our descendants.

① receive ② deserve ③ concern
④ preserve ⑤ surrender

2 The downside of the policy is that it is too expensive to implement.

① downturn ② drawback ③ downsizing
④ bottom side ⑤ effect

3 Delegates from 101 nations participated in the international event.

① clerks ② representatives ③ clients
④ donators ⑤ administrators

C 다음 주어진 단어를 알맞게 배열하여 우리말과 같은 뜻이 되도록 영작하시오.

1 현재 북극곰을 구하는 데 헌신하는 몇몇 조직이 있다.
(saving / currently / the polar bear / are / dedicated / there / several organizations / to)

→ ____

2 예를 들어 유전자 변형 식품이 얼마나 안전한지는 아무도 모른다.
(is / safe / knows /genetically modified food / nobody / for instance / really / how)

→ ____

3 그들은 그 매입을 주장했던 윌리엄 H. 수어드의 이름을 따서 그것을 이름 지었다.
(who / they / William H. Seward / it / , / insisted / after / the purchase / named)

→ ____

WORKBOOK

A 다음 빈칸에 알맞은 말을 <보기>에서 골라 쓰시오. (문맥에 맞는 어휘 고르기)

<보기> peak features mass-produce distance influential

1 The new menu ______________ several vegetarian dishes.

2 What is the ______________ between the Earth and Mars?

3 The singer was at the ______________ of his popularity in the late 1990s.

4 It was Henry Ford that began to ______________ cars.

5 He is an ______________ political figure in Korea.

B 글의 흐름으로 보아, 주어진 문장이 들어가기에 가장 적절한 곳을 고르시오. (문장 삽입)

It also takes place at the peak of the tomato harvesting season.

Have you ever heard about a strange Spanish festival called La Tomatina? It is an annual food fight festival held in the town of Buñol. Each year, up to 20,000 people participate in the world's largest food fight in the streets of the town. (①) The festival takes place on the last Wednesday of August. (②) In fact, nearly 140 tons of overripe tomatoes are transported into the city for the festival. Once the ceremonial rocket is fired into the air, the food fight begins. (③) The fight lasts for one full hour! Afterward, the streets are filled with tomato juice. (④) Storekeepers use huge plastic covers to protect their storefronts from the huge mess. (⑤) The festival is a week-long celebration that features music, parades, dancing, and fireworks. It attracts lots of tourists from all over the world. This festival gives a new meaning to the expression "playing with your food."

정답 p.30

C 음원을 듣고 빈칸을 채우시오. (지문뽀개기-받아쓰기)

Unit 01-02

Andy Warhol is one of the most __________ __________ of the twentieth century. He was often very ill when he was a child, so he spent a lot of time __________ __________ in bed. When he got older, he studied __________ __________ in college. He eventually moved to New York City in the 1960s, and there he began creating some of the world's __________ __________ __________. Warhol loved popular culture. He painted large pictures of Coca-Cola bottles, Campbell's soup cans, and dollar bills. He also __________ __________. He was one of the first painters to __________ __________ __________. Many criticized him for turning art into a business. Some people were unhappy because they thought he was just __________ __________ of the same picture, and they felt he was only interested in __________ __________. However, Warhol __________ __________ what he was doing, and he continued to create his own style of art until his death in 1987.

Unit 01-03

It is a common myth that the sky is blue because of a reflection of the __________ __________ __________. But it is not true at all. In fact, __________ __________ from the sun spreads around much more than all the other colors from the sun. That's what causes the sky __________ __________ __________.

Light is __________ __________ __________ electromagnetic waves, and the distance between two crests in this wave is called __________ __________. Red light, for instance, has the longest wavelength. The wavelength of blue light is __________ __________ __________ of red light. This difference in wavelength causes blue light to be scattered __________ __________ __________ more than red light. Lord Rayleigh studied this phenomenon __________ __________, and that's why it is commonly called as "Rayleigh scattering." There are some scientists, however, who call this "the Tyndall effect."

A 다음 빈칸에 알맞은 말을 <보기>에서 골라 쓰시오. 문맥에 맞는 어휘 고르기

<보기> thrived rejected indigenous enormous distracted

1 The temple is so ______________ that you cannot tour the entire place in one visit.

2 I was ______________ by the construction noise.

3 The country ______________ under the king's rule.

4 I offered some suggestions to my boss, but they were ______________.

5 That strange-looking bird is ______________ to Australia.

B 주어진 글 다음에 이어질 글의 순서로 가장 적절한 것을 고르시오. 글의 순서

Are you afraid of snakes? If so, you might want to consider relocating to New Zealand. This island in the South Pacific Ocean is completely free of land snakes. In fact, the island has only a small number of indigenous animals including bats, lizards, and frogs. For millions of years, New Zealand was isolated, which allowed many unique species of animals to thrive on the island.

(A) To protect the indigenous animals, the authorities in New Zealand impose strict regulations on the import of animals, and there are heavy penalties for illegally importing any plants or animals into New Zealand.

(B) For example, a shy and flightless bird called kiwi is one of New Zealand's best-known inhabitants. When European settlers arrived on the island, they brought many species of animals with them, such as dogs, deer, rabbits, pigs, and mice.

(C) Among them, a few have seriously impacted New Zealand's ecosystem, driving many other species to extinction. For instance, the kiwi, which once numbered in the millions, is now an endangered species.

① (A) – (C) – (B) ② (B) – (A) – (C) ③ (B) – (C) – (A)
④ (C) – (A) – (B) ⑤ (C) – (B) – (A)

정답 p. 30

C 음원을 듣고 빈칸을 채우시오. (지문뽀개기-받아쓰기)

Unit 02-01

The Palace of Versailles, __________ __________ __________, is the royal house of France. Originally, it was only a small hunting lodge, but King Louis XIV had an enormous expansion constructed __________ __________ __________. The Palace of Versailles became a symbol of his power. It also __________ __________ __________ __________ of the Royal Court. King Louis XIV held parties at the palace. These parties distracted many of the nobles from __________ __________ for performing their duties, which allowed King Louis XIV to rule France without __________ __________ __________ __________. The Palace's luxuries were so expensive that a lot of money was needed to __________ __________ __________. In addition, the palace also had a huge staff dedicated to __________ __________ __________ and his guests. In fact, twenty-five percent of France's __________ __________ was used to pay for the extravagances in the palace. Now the palace is used as a National Museum, and in 1979 it was named a World Heritage Site.

Unit 02-03

There was a chief living in Dagomba. He was very rich and had many __________ __________ __________. According to the traditions of those times, a man's __________ were not given to his son. Instead they were given to __________ __________. The chief wondered if his nephew would __________ __________ __________ __________ the possessions. As the chief's life was ending, he told his nephew, "When I am dead, select one thing that I own and take it. __________ __________ I will leave to my head slave. He has been very loyal and __________ __________ __________ all my life. I want you to inherit __________." The nephew thought at first, "My uncle rejects me, so I want __________ __________ __________ at all." His mother, however, told him that perhaps there was __________ __________ in it that he did not understand.

After his uncle's death, the nephew asked only for __________ __________ __________ and gave him a field and a house.

A 다음 빈칸에 알맞은 말을 <보기>에서 골라 쓰시오. (문맥에 맞는 어휘 고르기)

<보기> emerge observe face repetitive threat

1 In March, these bears _______________ from a long period of hibernation.

2 He wants to quit the job because the work is too _______________.

3 Chuseok and Sollnal are the two most important holidays that most Koreans _______________.

4 I was not brave enough to _______________ the danger.

5 It is not right to use violence and _______________ to get what you want.

B 글의 흐름으로 보아, 주어진 문장이 들어가기에 가장 적절한 곳을 고르시오. (문장 삽입)

This includes music, literature, architecture, and even philosophy.

Following the Second World War, a new form of art began to emerge. It was called minimalism. (①) This term refers to artwork that emphasizes extreme simplicity of form by using essential elements. (②) For instance, minimalist artists use only a few colors in their paintings. Another feature of this type of artwork can be seen in its appearance. (③) Many minimalist painters use simple geometric designs, such as squares or rectangles. Frank Stella was one of the first artists who used minimalist concepts in their artwork. (④) Several of his paintings are nothing more than stripes on a canvas. Minimalism can be found in many other forms of art as well. (⑤) Minimalist musicians use only simple melodies and rhythms in their songs, and the songs often contain many repetitive elements. Minimalism continued through the seventies and made a great impact on postmodern art.

정답 p. 30

C 음원을 듣고 빈칸을 채우시오. 지문뽀개기-받아쓰기

Unit 03-02

My grandfather was a veteran of the Second World War. He __________ __________ __________, but he had to watch many of his friends __________ __________ __________. Although he used to tell me that he was very proud of __________ __________ he provided for his country, he looked moody when Memorial Day arrived each year. Since the year my grandfather __________ __________, I have observed this holiday alone. Whenever I attend the __________ __________ in my hometown, I miss him terribly.
In the United States, Memorial Day is a __________ __________ for all to honor the men and women who __________ __________ __________ defending their country. Each year cities around the U.S. organize special ceremonies, parades, festivals, and other events to __________ __________ __________. The services honor all those who died __________ __________ __________ the U.S. Memorial Day began to be celebrated after the American Civil War, and it is now __________ __________.

Unit 03-03

People all around the world have loved rhino horns for more than 1,000 years. Many people in Africa, Europe, Arab, China, and India __________ __________ a rhino to use its horn. The horns __________ __________ __________ make status symbols and powerful medicines. In Africa some tribes used rhino horns as weapons, a tool, and a __________ __________ __________. Europeans started to become interested in rhino horns in the 19th century. They __________ __________ to make the tops of walking sticks and door handles. In Yemen, an Arab country, rich people have used rhino horns for __________ __________ for centuries. And in China, rhino horns are still used to this day __________ __________. Although all rhino species face __________ __________ __________ __________ in the wild, people still desire their horns.

A 다음 빈칸에 알맞은 말을 <보기>에서 골라 쓰시오. (문맥에 맞는 어휘 고르기)

<보기> administrative autonomy relinquish identified innocent

1 My job is mostly ______________.

2 I was forced to ______________ my position.

3 The local people have fiercely fought to gain ______________ for the region.

4 The old man was ______________ as her father.

5 The person accused of the theft turned out to be ______________.

B 주어진 글 다음에 이어질 글의 순서로 가장 적절한 것을 고르시오. (글의 순서)

A cow burps about 280 liters of methane every day. That doesn't seem very important to us, but the methane that cows burp up is dangerous for our environment.

(A) The bottom line: Every time a cow belches, it is contributing to global warming and the melting of the polar ice caps.

(B) Around the world, this number increases up to 80 million tons, when sheep, goats and buffalos are included. Carbon dioxide is the major greenhouse gas, but methane is 21 times more effective at trapping heat in the atmosphere.

(C) Methane is a greenhouse gas, and global warming is related to greenhouse gases. In the United States alone, every year about six million tons of cows' methane go up toward the sky.

① (A) – (C) – (B) ② (B) – (A) – (C) ③ (B) – (C) – (A)
④ (C) – (A) – (B) ⑤ (C) – (B) – (A)

정답 p. 30

C 음원을 듣고 빈칸을 채우시오. 지문뽀개기-받아쓰기

Unit 04-01

Macau is a __________ __________ __________ of the People's Republic of China. The Macau Peninsula is located to the west of Hong Kong and includes the small islands of Taipa and Coloane. Its civilization __________ __________ for over 6,000 years.
However, when the Portuguese arrived in the sixteenth century, they made Macau __________ __________ in the far East. Merchant ships used it as a __________ __________ for various goods.
This post allowed merchants to __________ __________ __________ __________ between China and the Western world. The Portuguese considered Macau to be an __________ __________ for a long period of time.
However, they eventually agreed to __________ __________ __________ to the People's Republic of China. On December 20, 1999, Portugal agreed to __________ __________ of Macau. It is presently considered a part of China, but it also enjoys a __________ __________ __________ __________ in many of its political matters.

Unit 04-02

Do you know __________ __________ in the United States on September 11, 2001? Four planes __________ __________ by terrorists, and two of those planes hit the Twin Towers of the World Trade Center in New York City. Every passenger __________ __________ the two airplanes was killed. A third plane __________ __________ into the Pentagon. Some brave passengers on a fourth plane managed to __________ __________ __________ before crashing into a field in Pennsylvania.
That day, everyone was __________ __________ their television screens as the incidents took place. Osama Bin Laden __________ __________ as the man who ordered these attacks. Soon after, President George W. Bush declared a __________ __________ __________. Actually, these suicide attacks killed almost three thousand __________ __________. All nineteen hijackers, Middle Eastern religious fanatics, were also killed. Americans felt a large amount of __________ __________ __________ after the tragedy. __________ __________ __________ __________ memorialize, they started to construct a new building on the same site __________ the Twin Towers used to stand and opened the building in 2014. The new building, which has 104 floors, is now called One World Trade Center and is a symbol of hope and victory for __________ __________ U.S. citizens __________ __________ peace-loving people around the world.

A 다음 빈칸에 알맞은 말을 <보기>에서 골라 쓰시오. (문맥에 맞는 어휘 고르기)

<보기> majority afford belongs passenger average

1 That textbook ________________ to Peter.

2 There was only one ________________ on the bus.

3 We cannot ________________ to travel to Europe right now.

4 ________________ middle school students would find this question too difficult.

5 The overwhelming ________________ of the voters oppose the policy.

B 글의 흐름으로 보아, 주어진 문장이 들어가기에 가장 적절한 곳을 고르시오. (문장 삽입)

The cost of traveling into space as a passenger on a spaceship is almost thirty-five million dollars.

After the first person landed on the Moon in 1969, people began to wonder how space travel would change our lives. Would people live on the Moon? When could the average person travel into space? Well, nobody lives on the Moon, yet. But people are finally beginning to travel into space. (①) Space tourism is a new phenomenon which is growing very quickly. (②) It gives people an opportunity to travel into space. Unfortunately, those opportunities are very expensive right now. (③) However, some companies want to start creating spaceships that can take tourists into space less expensively. New space stations are being built. (④) There have even been attempts to begin building a hotel in space! (⑤) Unfortunately, it may still take a long time before the average person can afford to take his or her vacation in the stars.

C 음원을 듣고 빈칸을 채우시오. (지문뽀개기-받아쓰기)

Unit 05-01

How often do you ________ ________ ________ in your life?
If you're like most people, you probably complain about your problems ________ ________ ________ ________. A lot of people find it easier to complain than ________ ________ ________ ________. Does this sound like you? Then you should do some research on the Complaint-Free World Project.
It's a very simple idea, and it may change your life! Several researchers believe that it takes twenty-one days to ________ ________ ________ ________. To begin the experiment, wear a purple wristband on your right wrist. Your goal is to be wearing it on ________ ________ ________ for twenty-one days.
However, if you complain, gossip about, or criticize someone, then you must move the bracelet ________ ________ ________ ________ and start all over again. So stop complaining! You just ________ ________ ________ about yourself.

Unit 05-03

There are around 6,800 different languages all around the world. Almost half of these languages, however, ________ ________ as a result of the loss of the cultures that speak them. What are these endangered languages and why do they disappear?
An endangered language is a language with nearly no one who speaks ________ ________ ________. Endangered languages belong to ________ ________ ________. Cultures are best passed on to ________ ________ through their languages, and cultures are lost when ________ ________ ________ ________. Sadly, thousands of languages have already disappeared, and they are disappearing more quickly, now. About 50% of the world's languages ________ ________. Many scholars worry that 90% of them will probably disappear ________ ________ ________ ________ two languages a month.
________ ________ to the loss of a language? Reasons such as these: the growth of cities, worldwide communication, and westernization, ________, ________, and so on. These make people who belong to small communities feel ashamed to ________ ________ their languages. Also, many people believe that children speaking a majority language have a ________ ________ for future success.

A 다음 빈칸에 알맞은 말을 <보기>에서 골라 쓰시오. (문맥에 맞는 어휘 고르기)

<보기> declared decorated sponsored inspired concern

1 The room was ________________ with balloons and flowers.

2 The government ________________ war on poverty.

3 His latest film was ________________ by his own experience.

4 The sports event is ________________ by some large businesses.

5 They have expressed ________________ that the project might not be practical.

B 주어진 글 다음에 이어질 글의 순서로 가장 적절한 것을 고르시오. (글의 순서)

Fresco painting is a picture that is painted on a wall while the plaster is still wet. During the Renaissance in Europe, this technique was very popular, and many artists used it to decorate buildings and church vaults.

(A) One of the most famous fresco painters was Diego Rivera. He inspired a revival of this art form in Mexico. Born in 1886, Diego studied art in Mexico. He traveled to Europe in 1907 to continue his study of art. Once he returned to Mexico, the government agreed to sponsor his work.

(B) Even though his work was not welcomed by everyone, he made an impact on America's public art scene. In 1957, at the age of seventy, Rivera died in Mexico City. To this day, he is still one of Mexico's most beloved painters.

(C) He painted a number of murals that depict scenes from Mexican history. Diego Rivera also worked in the United States. He painted murals for the City Club of the San Francisco Stock Exchange and the California School of Fine Art, and he once drew a communist picture of Lenin on the RCA Building at the Rockefeller Center in Manhattan. This created a lot of controversy for the artist, and his mural was destroyed shortly afterward.

① (A) – (C) – (B) ② (B) – (A) – (C) ③ (B) – (C) – (A)
④ (C) – (A) – (B) ⑤ (C) – (B) – (A)

정답 p. 31

C 음원을 듣고 빈칸을 채우시오. (지문뽀개기-받아쓰기)

Unit 06-01

Many winter festivals are held in countries throughout the world. However, __________ __________ __________ are as impressive as the Sapporo Snow Festival in Japan. __________ __________ __________ in February, the city is decorated with hundreds of beautiful snow statues and __________ __________. Artists come together to display a huge variety of sculptures. These include famous buildings, people, and __________ __________. They must possess a great deal of skill to __________ __________ __________ properly. They must know how to use a variety of tools such as chain saws and small chisels. At night, the ice sculptures __________ __________ __________ a dazzling display of colored lights. The festival also includes musical performances and delicious food. You can __________ __________ seafood, potatoes, corn, and fresh dairy products. There is even a beauty contest held each year. The winner is declared the Susukino Queen of Ice. Every year about __________ __________ __________ are created, and two million people visit Sapporo to enjoy the distinctive festival.

Unit 06-03

Hello, everyone. I am Dr. Lee at the Ministry of Health and Welfare. Today, I want to share the result of our latest surveys of __________ __________ in Korea. We found that the number of teenage smokers has increased a lot, to __________ __________ __________. I will report the main motivation of teenagers starting smoking, why it is so serious a matter, and what should be done about this.
First, friends can have __________ __________ over teenagers' lives. This is called "__________ __________" and this pressure can cause teenagers to start smoking. Second, teenagers begin to smoke because usually __________ __________ __________ about it. Also, students are affected by __________. They usually want to __________ like their favorite actors or singers and when they see them smoking, teenagers think they look cool.
Then, why is teenage cigarette smoking such a serious concern? Studies show that __________ __________ a teen begins smoking, __________ __________ __________ it is to break the nicotine addiction. Unfortunately, one-in-three teens who become __________ __________ will die early as a result of smoking, and half of all teens who smoke will eventually die __________ __________ __________ __________ tobacco-related illnesses.

A 다음 빈칸에 알맞은 말을 <보기>에서 골라 쓰시오. 문맥에 맞는 어휘 고르기

<보기> normal launched declined determine glacial

1 The police are trying to ______________ the cause of the fire.

2 We ______________ an attack against the enemy at midnight.

3 The ______________ period refers to the time when much of the northern hemisphere was covered with ice.

4 A certain degree of test anxiety is ______________ and helps students remain focused on their tests.

5 The illiteracy rate in the country has ______________ by 20% thanks to improved public education.

B 글의 흐름으로 보아, 주어진 문장이 들어가기에 가장 적절한 곳을 고르시오. 문장 삽입

Several factors contributed to the French Revolution.

The French Revolution, which began in 1789 and lasted for about ten years, was an important event in Western history. (①) Ultimately, the revolution caused the downfall of the monarchy's power in France. (②) Prior to the revolution, the quality of life in Europe had been determined by family status. (③) If you were born into a poor family, your life would be one of poverty. (④) It was not possible to raise your status if you were poor. (⑤) Unfair tax laws left the poor without much money. Severe food shortages also caused a lot of hardship for the peasants. On the other hand, the wealthy enjoyed a life of comfort, and the monarchy did not seem to care about the fate of the peasantry. The peasantry became terribly resentful of the wealthy aristocracy. They wanted greater equality in French society, and in 1789 they finally launched a violent political revolution which changed France's political landscape and gave political power to the people of France.

정답 p. 31

C 음원을 듣고 빈칸을 채우시오. 지문뽀개기-받아쓰기

Unit 07-02

Have you ever come __________ with a giant wooly mammoth? If you have, then it must have been inside a museum because this magnificent beast is __________ __________. The wooly mammoth was one of the largest creatures that had ever __________ __________ __________. It often grew to be sixteen-feet tall and __________ between six and eight tons. Why don't these animals __________ the Earth now? About 10,000 years ago, the number of wooly mammoths __________ __________ __________, and by around 1,600 B.C., __________ __________ __________ __________ of this species died out. Many researchers have concluded that __________ __________ was a significant factor. 12,000 years ago, the Earth's climate began to heat up, so icy regions of land around the world __________ __________ __________. This phenomenon is called "glacial retreat," and it drastically reduced the wooly mammoth's __________ __________. Another factor that contributed to the extinction of the wooly mammoth was __________ __________. The spread of advanced human hunters was likely a major cause of the mammoth's extinction. In fact, scientists have discovered cave drawings that illustrate __________ __________ __________ __________.

Unit 07-03

The first hole in the __________ __________ was found in 1984. Scientists discovered that the amount of ozone above Antarctica was much __________ __________ __________. Since then other ozone holes were found over other parts of the world. Why does it matter?

The ozone layer is important because it protects us from __________ __________ __________ that comes from the sun. This ultraviolet light called UV-B, is bad for people, animals, and plants. It can __________ __________, hurt animals' eyes and also reduce the growth rate of some plants.

The holes in the ozone layer are caused by __________ __________ __________ __________. These gases are called CFCs (chlorofluorocarbons). They are found in refrigerators, in __________ __________ __________ __________, aerosols, etc. Other gases called halons that are used in __________ __________ also make holes in the ozone layer. The only possible solution to the problem is using and making __________ __________ that contain CFCs or halons.

A 다음 빈칸에 알맞은 말을 <보기>에서 골라 쓰시오. 문맥에 맞는 어휘 고르기

<보기> landscape equator revenue purchased depicting

1 The city lies close to the ________________.

2 We ________________ some souvenirs at a gift shop.

3 The project didn't start to generate ________________ until 2018.

4 The photographer took a picture of the ________________ of the village.

5 The old cathedral has many murals ________________ scenes from the Bible.

B 주어진 글 다음에 이어질 글의 순서로 가장 적절한 것을 고르시오. 글의 순서

Boxing Day is one of the best shopping days of the year. It takes place on December 26, just after Christmas. For many stores, Boxing Day generates the highest revenues of the year. They often sell their products at highly discounted prices.

(A) However, Boxing Day can also make people a little bit crazy. Once inside, they often rush around and grab whatever they can. They even get into fights over merchandise!

(B) This attracts huge crowds of people. Stores are always full of shoppers on Boxing Day. Sometimes, people even wait outside of stores before they open. They have a good chance to get products at the lowest prices. They hope to purchase cheap televisions, clothes, or furniture.

(C) Boxing Day sales have the potential to create customer stampedes, injuries, and even fatalities. In order to protect customers, they often limit the number of people who are allowed inside.

① (A) – (C) – (B) ② (B) – (A) – (C) ③ (B) – (C) – (A)
④ (C) – (A) – (B) ⑤ (C) – (B) – (A)

정답 p. 31

C 음원을 듣고 빈칸을 채우시오. 지문뽀개기-받아쓰기

Unit 08-01

Impressionist artwork __________ __________ __________ during the nineteenth century. Impressionism was a __________ __________ from traditional artwork. Before Impressionism, artwork usually depicted royalty or religious figures, who were usually placed __________ __________ __________ of the painting. However, the background of the painting was not important. The introduction of Impressionism __________ __________ __________ __________ of what art was and how artwork was created. Artists began to focus on illustrating beautiful __________ __________. Impressionist artists often painted landscapes, people, and historical events. They used not only direct but reflected light to __________ __________ __________. This was very different from what most people were __________ __________ __________. Every part of the painting was important. Furthermore, the people that were depicted in the paintings were not always from a royal family. __________ __________ __________ __________! The subject of a painting could be a person walking in a park, or it could be __________ __________ in a tavern. Some famous impressionist painters include Renoir, Monet, and Degas.

Unit 08-03

Nowadays there are lots of disease, pollution, and war on Earth so people think that humans might live on __________ __________ sometime. Most planets are hotter than the places on the Earth's equator, colder than the Earth's __________ __________ __________ __________, or too far away for people to live. However, many scientists think that Mars might be a planet where people could live in the future. It would __________ __________ __________ __________ to travel to Mars, but it is still __________ __________ __________ to Earth. A short time ago the United States sent a spacecraft to Mars to search for water. Now it is proven that __________ __________ __________ on Mars. If there is water, then it might be possible __________ __________ __________ __________ there. This is important because all humans need water to live, and also, the water could be used __________ __________ __________ to return back to Earth. However, Mars can have __________ __________ __________ and not enough oxygen, which might make it difficult for people to live there. Would you like to go there sometime soon?

A 다음 빈칸에 알맞은 말을 <보기>에서 골라 쓰시오. 문맥에 맞는 어휘 고르기

<보기> operating underneath immigrant differs untimely

1 The machine was ________________ at high speeds making loud noise.

2 The city has a large ________________ population.

3 The cat quickly hid ________________ a car.

4 The ________________ death of the talented singer shocked his fans.

5 The second version ________________ greatly from the first one.

B 글의 흐름으로 보아, 주어진 문장이 들어가기에 가장 적절한 곳을 고르시오. 문장 삽입

However, both of these issues have been examined thoroughly, and the emergency staff in the tunnel are well-trained to handle any situations.

The Channel Tunnel is one of the most amazing feats of engineering in the world. Known as "The Chunnel," it operates between Great Britain and France. The tunnel is built underneath the English Channel. In fact, it is the longest undersea tunnel in the world. It was designed to make travel from Europe to the British Isles easier. (①) The idea for an underwater tunnel between England and France was initially suggested in 1802. (②) However, it was only in the 1980s that construction began on the project. Finally, the Chunnel officially opened in 1994. (③) There have been some problems in the underground tunnel since it opened. (④) Several small fires have stopped service in the tunnel. Initially, there was also a problem with illegal immigrants entering Britain. (⑤)

정답 p. 32

C 음원을 듣고 빈칸을 채우시오. (지문뽀개기-받아쓰기)

Unit 09-02

Who is the King of Pop? It's Michael Jackson! He __________ __________ through music videos, song writing, and live performances. Michael Jackson's musical career started at a __________ __________ __________. He was only eight years old when he became __________ __________ __________ of the Jackson 5. The Jackson 5 __________ __________ Michael and his brothers. Eventually, Michael began a solo career, and in the early 1980s he became the King of Pop. He wrote some of the __________ __________ __________ of all time. Songs such as Billie Jean and Thriller helped to make him a musical superstar.
However, on June 25, 2009, news of the __________ __________ __________ shocked the world. He had suffered from a __________ __________. Michael was taking several different medications at the time of his death. They included several types of __________. Doctors said that __________ __________ __________ administered by his personal physician __________ __________ __________ in his untimely death.
Millions of fans around the world showed their love and support. They built memorials __________ __________ __________ Michael and sang his songs together. His memory will __________ __________ through his unforgettable music.

Unit 09-03

Who are the Amish? The Amish __________ is about 140,000 and they live in places like Lancaster County, Pennsylvania and Ontario, Canada. The Amish are famous for __________ __________ __________ and keeping their lifestyle __________ __________ __________ __________. They believe __________ everything written in the Bible. They believe that they should __________ __________ __________ from the larger society.
Their lifestyle __________ __________ other modern people's. Amish men wear black suits, black shoes and straw broad-brimmed hats. Amish women wear solid-colored dresses with a __________ __________ __________. Many Amish couples have __________ __________ __________ children. Amish children go to school until they finish __________ __________ __________. Amish people don't think the modern technology helps to __________ __________ __________.
Lately, many tourists visit Amish communities and observe their __________ __________ of living.

A 다음 빈칸에 알맞은 말을 <보기>에서 골라 쓰시오. (문맥에 맞는 어휘 고르기)

<보기> numerous elected named strategic effort

1 She is very outgoing and has ______________ friends.

2 He ______________ his dog after his favorite actor.

3 She was ______________ as the mayor of New York.

4 The peninsular has great ______________ importance.

5 They all put a lot of ______________ into making a great movie.

B 주어진 글 다음에 이어질 글의 순서로 가장 적절한 것을 고르시오. (글의 순서)

Did you know that February 27 is International Polar Bear Day?

(A) You can also help by making an effort to conserve energy and by using public transportation to reduce your carbon footprint. Slowing global warming will help to preserve the polar bear's natural habitat. Even the smallest changes can make a huge difference!

(B) There are currently several organizations dedicated to saving the polar bear. They include the National Wildlife Federation and Polar Bears International. Each monetary donation to these organizations will be put toward helping save polar bears.

(C) Polar bears were the first species to become endangered because of climate change. The warmer the climate gets, the more the ice in the Arctic will melt. This poses a significant threat to the polar bear's home and its survival. If you want to help protect the polar bear, there are numerous ways for you to contribute.

① (A) – (C) – (B) ② (B) – (A) – (C) ③ (B) – (C) – (A)
④ (C) – (A) – (B) ⑤ (C) – (B) – (A)

C 음원을 듣고 빈칸을 채우시오. (지문뽀개기-받아쓰기)

Unit 10-02

Scientists have the __________ __________ __________ some truly amazing things nowadays. Did you know that they can __________ __________ our food? It's true. In the past, farmers have used traditional __________ __________ to grow their crops.
They would do this by harvesting seeds from their __________ __________. Then, they would plant those seeds the next year. This method, which is used to __________ __________ __________ and the quantity of crops, is called __________. Even though they come from their best crops, this method of breeding had __________ __________.
Scientists have found ways to break those limits. They can modify crops to make them __________ __________ to bacteria, viruses, and pests. This helps to reduce the quantity of __________ farmers use to protect their crops. In addition, modifying seeds can help them produce a larger quantity of crops. However, there is also a downside. For instance, nobody knows __________ __________ genetically modified food really is. There have not been any experiments designed to test the __________ __________ of genetically modified food.

Unit 10-03

U.S. bought Alaska from Russia for 7 million dollars in 1867. Most Americans thought it was a big mistake and __________ __________ __________. They called Alaska "Seward's Folly" or "Seward's Icebox." They __________ __________ __________ William H. Seward, the Secretary of State of the United States, who __________ the purchase.
However, __________ __________ __________ between 1896 and 1902, and whole cities grew almost __________. By then, many Alaskans fought for __________ __________, but the government ignored them. During World War II, in 1941, America declared war on Japan, and Alaska's __________ __________ became very important. The U.S. government began to __________ __________ its statehood.
Alaskans elected delegates, who met President Eisenhower. They convinced him to sign the Alaska Statehood Act in 1958. Finally, on January 3, 1959 Alaska became the __________ __________ of the United States of America.

MEMO

LEVEL CHART

초1 | 초2 | 초3 | 초4 | 초5 | 초6 | 중1 | 중2 | 중3 | 고1 | 고2 | 고3

VOCA

- 초등필수 영단어
  1-2 · 3-4 · 5-6학년용
- The VOCA + (플러스) 1~7
- THIS IS VOCABULARY
  입문 · 초급 · 중급
- 고급 · 어원 · 수능 완성 · 뉴텝스
- WORD FOCUS
  중등 종합 5000 · 고등 필수 5000 · 고등 종합 9500

Grammar

- 초등필수 영문법 + 쓰기
  1~2
- OK Grammar 1~4
- This Is Grammar Starter
  1~3
- This Is Grammar
  초급~고급 (각 2권: 총 6권)
- Grammar 공감 1~3
- Grammar 101 1~3
- Grammar Bridge 1~3 (NEW EDITION)
- The Grammar Starter, 1~3
- 한 권으로 끝내는 필수 구문 1000제
- 구사일생
  (구문독해 Basic) 1~2
- 구문독해 204 1~2 (개정판)
- 고난도 구문독해 500
- 그래머 캡처 1~2
- [특급 단기 특강]
  어법어휘 모의고사

READING 101

한번에 끝내는 중등 영어 독해

LEVEL 3

넥서스영어교육연구소 지음

정답 및 해설

NEXUS Edu

정답 및 해설

01 | FESTIVALS p.13

1 ③

2 ⓑ 8월의 마지막 수요일
ⓒ 싸움은 꼬박 한 시간 동안 지속된다!

3 ⑤ 4 ②

라 토마티나라고 불리는 색다른 스페인의 축제를 들어 본 적이 있는가? 그것은 부뇰 마을에서 열리는 연례 푸드 파이트(음식을 집어던지며 노는 싸움) 축제이다. 매년 2만 명에 이르는 사람들이 이 마을 거리에서 열리는 세계 최대의 푸드 파이트에 참가한다. 축제는 8월 마지막 수요일에 열린다. 그것은 토마토 수확의 절정기에 열리는 것이기도 하다. 실제로 약 140톤의 너무 익은 토마토를 이 축제를 위해 도시로 공수한다. 일단 기념 로켓이 공중으로 발사되면 푸드 파이트가 시작된다. 싸움은 꼬박 한 시간 동안 지속된다! 그런 다음에는 거리가 토마토 주스로 가득 찬다. 가게 주인들은 난장판으로부터 가게 앞을 보호하기 위하여 커다란 플라스틱 덮개를 사용한다. 축제는 음악, 퍼레이드, 춤, 불꽃놀이 등이 펼쳐지는 일주일간의 축하의식이다. 이 축제는 전 세계로부터 많은 관광객을 끌어들인다. 이 축제는 "음식을 가지고 놀기"라는 표현에 새로운 의미를 부여한다.

| 문제 해설 |

1 Have you ever heard about은 현재완료 중 경험을 의미한다. ①번은 결과, ②번은 완료 ③번은 경험, ④번은 계속, ⑤번도 계속이다.
① 제인은 선글라스를 잃어버렸다.
② 나는 이제 막 수필 쓰는 것을 끝마쳤다.
③ 나는 내 생애에서 그렇게 무서워 본 적이 없다.
④ 토마스는 유나와 결혼한 이후로 서울에서 살고 있다.
⑤ 레베카는 3년 동안 중학교에서 영어를 가르치고 있다.

2 ⓑ의 last는 '마지막의'라는 의미의 형용사로 쓰였고, ⓒ의 lasts는 '지속하다'라는 의미의 동사로 쓰였다.

3 축제에서 토마토를 가지고 노는 내용이므로 빈칸에는 playing with가 가장 적절하다.
윗글의 빈칸 (A)에 들어갈 말로 가장 적절한 것은?
① ~을 팔기
② ~을 요리하기
③ ~을 심기
④ ~을 위해 싸우기
⑤ ~을 가지고 놀기

4 축제기간에 라 토마티나 참가자들이 토마토를 수확하는 것이 아니라, 라 토마티나가 토마토 수확이 한창인 시즌에 개최되는 것이다.
① 라 토마티나는 일 년에 한 번 열린다.
② 라 토마티나 동안 참가자들은 토마토를 수확한다.
③ 라 토마티나를 위해 많은 토마토가 사용된다.
④ 사람들은 라 토마티나에서 토마토 싸움을 포함에서 다른 이벤트를 즐길 수 있다.
⑤ 라 토마티나는 일주일 동안 지속된다.

| 영영풀이 |

1 harvest: ~을 수확하다, 거둬들이다
2 transport: ~을 운송하다, 수송하다
3 mess: 엉망진창

| 구문풀이 |

9행 **Once** the ceremonial rocket ~ is fired into the air.
once는 '일단 ~하면, ~하자마자'라는 의미로 부사절을 이끄는 접속사이다.

12행 The festival is *a week-long celebration* **that** features music, parades, dancing, and fireworks.
that 이하는 주격 관계대명사절로 선행사 a week-long celebration을 수식한다.

02 | PEOPLE p.15

1 ① 2 ③ 3 popular culture

앤디 워홀은 20세기에 가장 영향력 있는 예술가 중 한 명이다. 그는 어릴 적에 자주 아파서 침대에 누워 그림을 그리며 많은 시간을 보냈다. 나이가 들고 그는 대학에서 미술을 공부했다. 마침내 그는 1960년대에 뉴욕으로 이주하여 그곳에서 세계에서 가장 유명한 미술작품을 창작하기 시작했다. 워홀은 대중문화를 사랑했다. 그는 커다란 코카콜라 병과 캠벨의 수프 깡통, 달러 지폐를 그렸다. 그는 또한 유명 인사들을 그렸다. 그는 자신의 작품을 대량 생산한 최초의 화가 중 한 명이었다. 많은 사람이 예술을 상업으로 바꿔 버렸다고 그를 비난했다. 어떤 사람들은 그가 단지 같은 그림을 복사해 내고 있다는 생각에 불만스러워했다. 그리고 그들은 그가 오로지 돈벌이에만 관심이 있다고 생각했다. 하지만, 워홀은 자신이 하는 일에 신념이 있었으며, 1987년에 죽을 때까지 자신만의 스타일로 예술을 계속 창작했다.

| 문제 해설 |

1 앤디 워홀은 예술 작품을 처음으로 대량 생산한 예술가로 예술을 상업으로 바꾸었다는 비난을 받았다.
① 예술 … 상업
② 대중문화 … 큰 그림들
③ 상품들 … 훌륭한 예술
④ 패스트푸드 … 대중문화
⑤ 예술 … 단지 한 개의 그림

2 빈칸에는 believed in의 목적어가 되면서 he was doing의 목적어도 되는 선행사를 포함하는 관계대명사 what이 필요하다.

3 Coca-Cola bottles, Campbell's soup cans, dollar bills 등을 대표할 수 있는 단어는 popular culture(대중문화)이다.

| 영영풀이 |

1 popular: 대중적인
2 celebrity: 유명인, 명사
3 criticize: ~을 비판하다

| 구문풀이 |

1행 Andy Warhol is **one of the most influential artists** of the twentieth century.
「one of the+최상급+복수명사」는 '가장 ~한 것 중 하나'라고 해석한다. 「one of the+최상급+복수명사」가 주어로 나오면 단수동사가 온다.

3행 so he **spent** a lot of time **drawing** pictures in bed
spend+시간+-ing: ~하는 데 시간을 쓰다

9행 Many criticized him for **turning** art **into** a business.
turn A (in)to B: A를 B로 바꾸다

11행 because they **thought he** was just making copies of the same picture, and they **felt he** was only interested in making money
thought와 he 사이, felt와 he 사이에 각각 thought와 felt의 목적어절을 이끄는 접속사 that이 생략되어 있다.

03 | INTERESTING FACTS p.17

1 ③ 2 ④ 3 ②
4 reflection, blue light

하늘은 바다와 대양이 반사되어 푸르다라는 것이 일반적인 통념이다. 그러나 그것은 전혀 사실이 아니다. 사실, 태양에서 온 푸른 광선은 다른 색의 광선들에 비해 훨씬 더 넓게 퍼진다. 그것이 하늘이 푸르게 보이는 이유이다. 빛은 전자파로 이루어져 있고, 마루와 마루 사이의 거리를 파장이라고 부른다. 예를 들어, 붉은 광선은 가장 긴 파장을 가지고 있다. 푸른 광선의 파장은 붉은 광선의 절반 정도의 길이이다. 이 파장의 차이로 인해 푸른 광선이 붉은 광선에 비해 거의 10배 이상 자주 흩어진다. 레일리 경이 이 현상을 상세히 연구했는데, 그 때문에 이 현상은 '레일리 산란'라고 불린다. 그러나 어떤 과학자들은 이 현상을 '틴들 효과'라고 부른다.

| 문제 해설 |

1 앞의 문장과 대비되는 내용이 나오므로 however(그러나)로 연결해야 자연스럽다.

2 The wavelength of blue light is about half that of red light.에서 푸른 광선의 파장이 붉은 광선의 파장의 절반 정도의 길이라고 말하고 있으므로 ④의 '푸른 광선의 파장이 붉은 광선의 것보다 짧다.'는 말은 옳다.
① 빛은 파장으로 이루어져있다.
② 붉은 광선은 모든 다른 빛보다 더 많이 퍼진다.
③ 붉은 광선은 푸른 광선보다 거의 10배 더 퍼진다.
④ 푸른 광선의 파장은 붉은 광선보다 더 짧다.
⑤ 빛의 파장의 두 부분 사이의 공간을 전자파라고 한다.

3 레일리 경이 푸른 광선의 산란 현상을 연구했고 그 현상이 '레일리 산란'이라고 불렸다는 내용에서 레일리 경이 하늘이 파란 이유를 처음 알아낸 사람이라는 것을 알 수 있다.
① 지구 대기를 연구한 첫 번째 사람이었다.
② 하늘이 푸른 이유를 이해한 첫 번째 사람이었다.
③ 파장의 차이를 발견한 첫 번째 사람이었다.
④ 태양이 대기에 주는 영향을 연구한 첫 번째 사람이었다.
⑤ 대기에서 태양의 역할을 이해한 첫 번째 사람이었다.

4 비록 많은 사람들이 하늘이 푸른 이유는 지구의 물이 반사되기 때문이라고 생각하지만 실제로는 지구의 대기에서 흩어져서 생기는 푸른 광선의 파장 길이 때문이다.

| 영영풀이 |

1 reflection: 반사, 반영
2 crest: 마루, 정상
3 detail: 세부사항

| 구문풀이 |

1행 **It** is a common myth **that** the sky is blue because of a reflection of the seas and oceans.
it은 가주어, that이하는 진주어이다.

5행 Light **is made up of** electromagnetic waves, and the distance between two crests in this wave **is called** the wavelength.
be made up of는 '~으로 구성되다'의 의미로 쓰이는 수동태 표현이다. call은 목적어와 목적격 보어를 취하는 5형식 동사인데, 목적어(the distance between two crests in this wave)가 주어 자리로 나간 수동태형으로 쓰였다.

Review Test p.18

A

1 detail 2 celebrity
3 transport 4 criticize
5 reflection

B

1 ③ 2 ⑤ 3 ②

C

1 Once the ceremonial rocket is fired into the air, the food fight begins.
2 He spent a lot of time drawing pictures in bed.
3 That's what causes the sky to appear blue.

A

1 detail: 세부사항
2 celebrity: 유명인, 명사
3 transport: ~을 운송하다, 수송하다
4 criticize: ~을 비판하다
5 reflection: 반사, 반영

B

1 take place: 발생하다, 일어나다(= be held)
다음 영어 교육 회의는 10월에 열릴 것입니다.
2 influential: 영향력 있는(= powerful)
그녀는 21세기의 가장 영향력 있는 정치인 중 한 명이다.
3 be made up: 구성되다(= consist)
우리 드론 클럽은 5명의 학생들로 구성되어있다.

C

1 once+주어+동사: 일단 ~하면
2 spend+시간+-ing: ~하느라 시간을 보내다
3 관계사 what(= the thing which)

01 | PLACES p.21

1 ④ 2 the nobles
3 ③

1624년에 세워진 베르사유 궁은 프랑스의 궁전이다. 원래 그곳은 작은 사냥 별장이었으나, 국왕 루이 14세가 그의 재위 기간 중 거대한 확장 공사를 하게 했다. 베르사유 궁은 그의 권력의 상징이 되었다. 또한 그것은 왕실의 막대한 부를 과시했다. 루이 14세는 궁에서 파티를 열었다. 이런 파티가 귀족들의 관심을 의무 수행에 대한 책임감으로부터 다른 곳으로 돌리게 했고, 이로써 루이 14세는 그들의 간섭을 받지 않고 프랑스를 통치할 수 있게 되었다. 궁전의 사치품이 지나치게 비싸서 궁을 유지하려면 돈이 많이 필요했다. 게다가 베르사유 궁에는 왕과 왕의 손님의 시중을 드는 데 종사하는 엄청난 수의 시종이 있었다. 실제로 프랑스 국가 수입의 25%는 궁의 사치품 비용을 지급하는 데 사용되었다. 지금 궁은 국립박물관으로 사용되고 있으며, 1979년에는 세계문화유산으로 지정되었다.

| 문제 해설 |

1 (A) 확장 공사가 (공사하는 사람들에 의해서) 시행되는 것이므로 수동형인 constructed가 답이다. (B) allow는 목적격 보어로 to부정사를 취하므로 to rule이 답이다. (C) 프랑스 국가 수입의 25퍼센트가 사치품의 비용을 대는 데 사용되는 것이므로 was used to pay가 답이다.
2 them은 귀족들을 지칭한다.
3 베르사유 궁의 유지에 돈이 많이 드는 이유를 계속 열거하고 있으므로 빈칸에는 In addition(게다가)이 가장 적절하다.

| 영영풀이 |

1 demonstrate: 보여주다, 입증하다
2 vast: 방대한
3 dedicate: 헌신하다

| 구문풀이 |

3행 King Louis XIV **had** an enormous expansion (O) constructed (OC) during his reign.

had는 사역동사로 '~을 …하게 시키다'라는 의미를 갖는데 목적어와 목적격 보어의 관계가 능동이면 목적격 보어에 현재분사(또는 동사원형)를, 목적어와 목적격 보어의 관계가 수동이면 과거분사를 쓴다.
I had my car fixed. 나는 내 자동차를 수리시켰다.
(내 차가 수리되는 것: 수동)
He had us laughing. 그는 우리 모두를 웃게 했다.
(우리가 웃는 것: 능동)

He had me wait outside. 그는 나를 밖에서 기다리게 했다.
(내가 기다리는 것: 능동)

7행 *These parties distracted many of the nobles from taking responsibility for performing their duties,* **which** allowed King Louis XIV to rule France ~.
which는 계속적 용법의 주격 관계대명사로 앞 문장 전체를 선행사로 받으며, and it으로 바꿔 쓸 수 있다.

9행 The Palace's luxuries were **so** expensive **that** a lot of money was needed to maintain the palace.
so+형용사+that+주어+동사: 매우 ~해서 …하다

11행 the palace also had *a huge staff* **dedicated** to serving the king and his guests
dedicated 이하는 a huge staff를 수식한다. dedicated 앞에는 「관계대명사+be동사」가 생략되었다.

02 | ANIMALS

p.23

1 ⑤ 2 ② 3 European settlers
4 ②

뱀이 무서운가? 만일 그렇다면, 뉴질랜드로 이주하는 것을 생각해 보고 싶을지도 모른다. 남태평양에 있는 이 섬은 뱀이 전혀 없다. 사실 이 섬에는 박쥐와 도마뱀, 개구리를 포함해서 단지 적은 수의 토착 동물이 있을 뿐이다. 수백만 년 동안 뉴질랜드는 고립되어 있었고, 이 때문에 이 섬에는 많은 독특한 종의 동물이 번성했다. 예를 들어, 키위라 불리는 수줍음 많고 날지 못하는 새는 뉴질랜드의 가장 잘 알려진 토착 동물 중 하나이다. 유럽 정착민이 이 섬에 도착했을 때, 그들은 개, 사슴, 토끼, 돼지, 쥐 등 많은 종의 동물을 함께 데리고 왔다. 이들 중 몇몇 종은 뉴질랜드의 생태계에 심각한 영향을 미쳤고, 다른 종들을 멸종시켰다. 예를 들어, 키위는 한때 수백만 마리에 달했었는데 이제는 멸종 위기의 동물이 되었다. 토착 동물을 보호하기 위하여 뉴질랜드 정부 당국은 동물의 수입에 강력한 규제를 가하고 있고, 불법적으로 뉴질랜드에 들여오는 모든 식물과 동물에 무거운 벌금을 부과하고 있다.

| 문제 해설 |

1 윗글은 뉴질랜드에 사는 토착 동물에 관한 내용이다.
윗글의 제목으로 가장 적절한 것은?
① 살기 좋은 곳 뉴질랜드
② 뉴질랜드에 뱀이 없는 이유
③ 뉴질랜드 원주민의 역사
④ 뉴질랜드에서 동물을 기르는 방법
⑤ 뉴질랜드의 토착 동물

2 빈칸 (A) 뒤에 앞의 내용과 연결되어 좀 더 자세한 내용이 나오므로 빈칸 (A)에는 In fact가 적절하고, 빈칸 (C) 뒤에서는 멸종 위기에 처한 동물의 예시가 나오므로 빈칸 (C)에는 For instance가 적절하다.
① 하지만 … 게다가
② 사실 … 예를 들어
③ 그러므로 … 반면에
④ 게다가 … 더욱이
⑤ ~에도 불구하고 … 대조적으로

3 유럽 정착민이 뉴질랜드에 들어올 때 다른 동물들을 들여온 것이므로 them은 유럽 정착민을 지칭한다.
(B) them이 가리키는 것은 무엇인가?

4 ⓑ included가 아니라 '~을 포함하여'라는 뜻의 전치사 including이 필요하다.

| 영영풀이 |

1 isolated: 고립된
2 authority: 당국
3 impose: 부과하다, 지우다

| 구문풀이 |

2행 This island in the South Pacific Ocean is completely **free of** land snakes.
free of: ~이 없는, 면제된

4행 *New Zealand was isolated,* **which** allowed many unique species of animals to thrive on the island.
which는 앞 문장을 선행사로 받는 계속적 용법의 주격 관계대명사로 and it으로 바꿔 쓸 수 있다. allow는 to부정사를 목적격 보어로 취하며, '~가 …하는 것을 허락하다'라고 해석한다.

9행 a few have seriously impacted New Zealand's ecosystem, **driving** many other species to extinction
부대상황을 의미하는 분사구문으로 and have driven many other species to extinction으로 바꿔 쓸 수 있다.

11행 *the kiwi,* **which** once numbered in the millions, is now an endangered species
which는 the kiwi를 받는 계속적 용법의 주격 관계대명사이고, which가 이끄는 절이 the kiwi와 is사이에 삽입된 것이다.

03 | TALES FROM THE WORLD p.25

1 ④ 2 ④ 3 ③

다곰바에 족장이 한 명 살고 있었다. 이 사람은 굉장한 부자였고 많은 종과 노예를 거느리고 있었다. (a) 그 당시의 전통에 따르면, 남자의 재산은 자신의 아들에게 주어지지 않았다. 대신 그것은 조카에게 주어졌다. 족장은 자신의 조카가 재산을 잘 관리할지 궁금했다. 족장은 여생이 얼마 남지 않게 되자, 조카에게 이렇게 말했다. "내가 죽으면, 내가 가지고 있는 것 중에서 한 가지를 골라 그것을 가져라. 나머지는 모두 노예장에게 주겠다. 노예장은 평생 나에게 아주 충성했고, 신의를 지켰기 때문이다. 그러니 현명하게 유산을 상속받아라." 조카는 처음에는 이렇게 생각했다. "삼촌이 나를 저버렸으니까, 나는 아무 것도 받지 않을 거야." 그러나 어머니는 그 말에는 아마도 자기 아들이 이해하지 못하는 (b) 어떤 의미가 있을 것이라고 말해 주었다. 삼촌이 죽자 조카는 노예장만 달라고 요구했으며, 그 노예장에게 밭과 집을 주었다.

| 문제 해설 |

1 Instead they(= a man's possessions) were given to his nephew를 통해 남자의 재산을 조카가 받는 것이 '그 당시의 전통'임을 알 수 있다.
① 남자의 땅을 도시에 넘겨야 한다.
② 남자는 그의 유언을 계획해야 한다.
③ 남자의 조카는 자신의 딸과 결혼해야 한다.
④ 남자의 재산은 조카에게 주어진다.
⑤ 남자의 노예장은 충성해야 한다.

2 결국에는 조카가 어머니의 조언을 듣고 노예장을 소유하는 똑똑한 선택을 하는 내용이므로 족장이 조카가 현명하기를 바랐다는 것을 알 수 있다.
① 족장은 자신의 조카를 싫어했다.
② 족장은 아무 말도 할 수 없었다.
③ 족장은 노예장이 자신의 재산을 물려받기를 원했다.
④ 족장은 조카가 현명하기를 바랐다.
⑤ 족장은 자신의 조카에게 재산 전부를 물려주고 싶지는 않았다.

3 족장은 노예장에게 모든 재산을 주었고 조카는 노예장을 소유하게 되었으므로 결국 족장의 모든 재산은 조카에게 주어지는 것이나 마찬가지다.

| 영영풀이 |

1 possession: 재산, 소유물
2 inherit: 상속하다, 물려받다
3 reject: 버리다, 거절하다

| 구문풀이 |

2행 a man's possessions **were not given to** his son
4형식의 수동태 문장이며, 「직접목적어+be동사+p.p.+전치사(to/for)+간접목적어」 형태를 취하고 있다.

4행 The chief wondered **if** his nephew would take good care of the possessions.
의문사가 없는 간접의문문은 「if/whether+주어+동사」의 형식을 취한다.

6행 **Everything else** I will leave to my head slave.
Everything else는 원래 leave의 목적어로, leave 뒤에 위치하는 것이 일반적이나, 강조할 때는 문두로 나올 수 있다.

Review Test p.26

A

1 inherit 2 vast
3 possession 4 isolated
5 dedicate

B

1 ④ 2 ⑤ 3 ④

C

1 The palace also had a huge staff dedicated to serving the king and his guests.
2 There are heavy penalties for illegally importing any plants or animals into New Zealand.
3 The chief wondered if his nephew would take good care of the possessions.

A

1 inherit: 상속하다, 물려받다
2 vast: 방대한
3 possession: 재산, 소유물
4 isolated: 고립된
5 dedicate: 헌신하다

B

1 enormous: 막대한(= immense)
레이첼은 최근 엄청난 스트레스를 받아왔다.
2 indigenous: 토착의(= native)
캥거루는 호주가 원산지이다.
3 reject: 거절하다(= turn down)
1년 동안 여행을 하고 싶었던 그녀는 취업 제의를 거절했다.

C

1 a huge staff dedicated to serving ~
(= a huge staff that was dedicated to serving ~)
2 for: 이유를 나타내는 전치사
3 if(~인지 아닌지): 간접의문문을 만드는 명사절 접속사

01 | ART p.29

1 ③ 2 ⑤ 3 ①
4 단순한 멜로디와 리듬, 반복적인 요소

제2차 세계대전 이후 새로운 형태의 예술이 등장하기 시작했다. 그것은 미니멀리즘(최소 표현주의)라고 불렸다. 이 용어는 필수적 요소를 사용하여 극단적으로 간단한 형태를 강조하는 예술 작업을 말한다. 예를 들어 미니멀리즘 작가들은 그림에서 몇 가지의 색깔만을 사용한다. 이러한 형태의 예술 작품의 또 다른 특징은 그 외형에서도 볼 수 있다. 많은 미니멀리즘 화가는 정사각형이나 직사각형 같은 단순한 기하학적 디자인을 사용한다. 프랭크 스텔라는 예술작업에 미니멀리즘이라는 개념을 사용한 최초의 예술가 중 한 명이었다. 그의 몇몇 그림은 캔버스에 단지 줄을 쭉쭉 그은 것에 지나지 않는다. 미니멀리즘은 많은 다른 형태의 예술에서도 찾아볼 수 있다. 여기에는 음악과 문학, 건축, 심지어 철학까지도 포함된다. 미니멀리즘 음악가는 노래에 간단한 멜로디와 리듬만을 사용하고, (미니멀리즘) 노래에는 대개 반복적 요소가 많이 포함된다. 미니멀리즘은 70년대 내내 계속되었고 포스트모던 예술에 큰 영향을 주었다.

| 문제 해설 |

1 ⓐ that은 주격 관계대명사로 선행사인 artwork를 수식하는 절을 이끈다. ① that은 the news와 동격이 되는 절을 이끄는 접속사이다. ② that은 목적격 관계대명사로 선행사 The girl을 수식하는 절을 이끌고 saw의 목적어가 된다. ③ that은 주격 관계대명사로 선행사 My old friend를 수식하는 절을 이끈다. ④ that은 knew의 목적어절을 이끄는 접속사이다. ⑤ that은 bicycle을 수식하는 지시형용사이다.
① 그는 아마 그녀가 곧 이사한다는 소식을 듣지 못했을 것이다.
② 우리가 버스 정류장에서 본 소녀는 나의 반 친구다.
③ 일본에 사는 내 오랜 친구가 어젯밤에 나에게 전화했다.
④ 그는 그녀가 진실을 모른다는 것을 알았다.
⑤ 나는 2주 전에 그 자전거를 샀다.
2 미니멀리즘은 사물을 단순화해서 표현하는 기법이므로 빈칸에는 simple이 가장 적절하다.
① 복잡한
② 부드러운
③ 다양한
④ 호전적인
⑤ 단순한
3 사각형이나 선으로 표현된 단순한 그림이 미니멀리즘에 속한다.
4 simple melodies and rhythms와 repetitive elements라고 했으므로 단순한 멜로디와 리듬, 반복적인 요소가 답이다.

| 영영풀이 |

1 term: 용어
2 emphasize: 강조하다
3 essential: 중요한, 핵심적인

| 구문풀이 |

1행 **Following** the Second World War, a new form of art began to emerge.
전 following: ~에 이어, ~에 뒤따르는

9행 Frank Stella was one of *the first artists* **who** used minimalist concepts in their artwork.
who는 주격 관계대명사로 선행사 the first artists를 수식하는 절을 이끈다.

10행 Several of his paintings are **nothing more than** stripes on a canvas.
nothing more than: ~일 뿐이다, ~에 지나지 않는다

02 | SPECIAL DAYS p.31

1 ① 2 ④ 3 ① 4 ③

(A) 우리 할아버지는 제2차 세계대전의 참전용사였다. 그는 수많은 전쟁터에서 살아남았지만, 많은 전우가 전투에서 죽는 것을 지켜봐야 했다. 할아버지는 국가를 위해 한 일이 매우 자랑스럽다고 말씀하시곤 했지만, 매년 전몰장병 추모일(메모리얼 데이 / 현충일)이 되면 우울해 보이셨다. 할아버지가 돌아가신 그 해 이후부터는 나 혼자 이 기념일을 맞고 있다. 고향마을에서 추모 기념식에 참석할 때마다 나는 할아버지가 너무 그립다.
(B) 미국에서 모든 사람에게 있어 전몰장병 추모일은 조국을 지키는 데 목숨을 희생한 남녀를 기리는 슬픈 공휴일이다. 미국 전역의 도시들은 매년 이를 기념하기 위해 특별한 기념식과 퍼레이드, 페스티벌, 다른 이벤트를 마련한다. 그 기념식에서는 미국을 지키기 위하여 죽은 모든 사람을 추앙한다. 전몰장병 추모일은 남북전쟁 이후부터 시행되기 시작했으며, 지금은 미국 전역에서 지켜진다.

| 문제 해설 |

1 (A)에서 필자가 할아버지를 그리워하는 마음이 드러나므로 nostalgic이 가장 적절하다.
① (과거를) 그리워하는
② 신이 나는
③ 겁을 주는
④ 지루한
⑤ 긴장한

2 ⓐ의 when은 '~ 때'라는 의미로 시간 부사절을 이끄는 접속사이다. ① when은 '언제'라는 뜻의 의문사이다. ② when은 '언제'라는 뜻의 의문사이다. ③ It ~ that[when] 강조 용법에서 강조하는 말이 시간 부사면 that 대신 when을 쓸 수 있다. ④ when은 '~ 때'라는 의미로 시간 부사절을 이끄는 접속사이다. ⑤ when은 관계부사로 선행사 the day를 수식하는 절을 이끈다.
① 너는 언제 고향이 그립니?
② 그가 언제 올 건지 아니?
③ 우리가 만난 때는 바로 이른 아침이었다.
④ 나는 6학년 때 손목이 부러졌었다.
⑤ 1월 1일이 나의 첫 조카가 태어난 날이다.

3 (B)는 전몰장병 추모일에 관한 글로 설명문이다.

4 (A)에서 필자의 할아버지는 전쟁 중에 나라를 위해 하신 일을 자랑스러워하셨다.
① 할아버지는 제2차 세계대전 때 군인이었다.
② 전쟁터에서 할아버지의 전우들이 많이 죽었다.
③ 할아버지는 전쟁 중에 자신이 한 일에 대해 자랑스러워하지 않으셨다.
④ 미국의 전몰장병 추모일은 슬픈 기념일이다.
⑤ 전몰장병 추모일은 미국의 남북전쟁 이후로 지켜지기 시작했다.

| 영영풀이 |

1 combat: 전투
2 organize: 구성하다
3 defense: 방위, 방어

| 구문풀이 |

3행 Although he **used to** tell me **that** he was very proud of *the service* [he provided for his country], / he looked moody **when** Memorial Day arrived each year.

Although he ~ his country는 양보 부사절이고, that은 tell의 직접목적어절을 이끄는 접속사이다. used to는 과거의 습관을 나타내는 표현으로 '~하곤 했다'라고 해석한다. he provided for his country는 선행사 the service를 수식하는 목적격 관계대명사절이고, the service와 he 사이에 provided의 목적어가 되는 목적격 관계대명사 that[which]가 생략되어 있다. when은 '~ 때'라는 의미로 시간 부사절을 이끄는 접속사이다.

8행 **Whenever** I attend the memorial service ~.

Whenever는 '~할 때마다'라는 뜻으로 Every time when[that]으로 바꿔 쓸 수 있다.

11행 *a somber holiday* (for all) **to honor** *the men and women* **who** sacrificed their lives **defending** their country

to honor 이하는 a somber holiday를 수식하고, who 이하의 주격 관계대명사절은 선행사 the men and women을 수식한다. defending their country는 '나라를 지키는 데'라는 의미의 분사구문이다.

03 | ANIMALS

p.33

1 ④ 2 ② 3 ①
4 rhino horn

전 세계의 사람들이 지금까지 천년이 넘도록 코뿔소의 뿔을 아주 좋아했다. 아프리카, 유럽, 아랍, 중국, 인도에서는 뿔을 이용하려고 코뿔소를 사냥한 사람들이 많았다. 그 뿔은 사회적 신분을 나타내는 상징으로, 강력한 약효를 지닌 의약품으로 이용되었다. 아프리카에서는 코뿔소의 뿔을 무기, 도구, 행운의 부적으로 이용하는 부족들이 있다. 유럽인들은 19세기에 코뿔소의 뿔에 관심을 나타내기 시작했다. 이들은 지팡이의 머리 장식과 문의 손잡이를 만드는 데에 이것들을 사용했다. (오늘날에는 코뿔소의 뿔로 무엇이든 만드는 것은 불법이다.) 아랍 국가인 예멘에서는 부자들은 수백 년 동안 코뿔소의 뿔로 단검을 만들었다. 그리고 중국에서는 오늘날까지도 코뿔소의 뿔을 약재로 이용한다. 야생 상태에서 사는 코뿔소의 종들은 모두 멸종의 위협에 직면하고 있지만 사람들은 아직도 그 뿔을 가지고 싶어 한다.

| 문제 해설 |

1 예전부터 오늘날까지 코뿔소의 뿔이 사용되는 사례에 대한 내용 중에 오늘날에는 코뿔소의 뿔로 무엇이든 만드는 것은 불법이라는 내용은 흐름과 어울리지 않는다.

2 코뿔소의 뿔을 약재로 이용하는 것은 아프리카의 부족이 아니라 중국인이다.

① 중국인들은 코뿔소 뿔을 약재로 이용해 왔다.

② 일부 아프리카 부족은 코뿔소 뿔을 약으로 이용했다.

③ 유럽인은 19세기부터 코뿔소 뿔에 관심을 가졌다.

④ 아프리카인, 아랍인, 인도인을 포함해서 많은 사람들이 코뿔소 뿔을 원해 왔다.

⑤ 코뿔소 뿔은 유럽에서 지팡이 머리 장식에 이용되었다.

3 마지막 문장에 코뿔소의 종들이 모두 멸종 위기에 처해있다는 내용을 다루고 있으므로 사람들은 코뿔소의 사냥을 멈춰야 한다는 내용이 뒤따라야 자연스럽다.

① 사람들은 코뿔소 사냥을 멈춰야 한다.

② 정부는 사람들의 수요에 응하기 위해서 코뿔소를 많이 길러야 한다.

③ 뿔 이외에도 사람들이 코뿔소로부터 얻을 수 있는 이익은 많이 있다.

④ 코뿔소는 매우 커서 코뿔소를 화나게 하는 것은 위험하다.

⑤ 사람들은 코뿔소를 제외한 다른 동물을 사냥해야 한다.

4 코뿔소의 뿔은 여러 가지 용도로 쓰이기 때문에 전 세계적으로 천년이 넘는 세월 동안 가지고 싶어 하는 사람들이 많았다.

| 영영풀이 |

1 weapon: 무기

2 extinction: 멸종

3 desire: 갈망하다

| 구문풀이 |

3행 The horns **were used to make** status symbols and powerful medicines.

「be used to부정사」는 '~하는데 사용되다'는 의미로 쓰인다. 「be used to 동명사(~하는데 익숙하다)」와 헷갈리지 말자.

7행 Today, **it** is illegal **to use** rhino horns to make anything.

it은 가주어, to use이하는 진주어이다.

8행 In Yemen, an Arab country, rich people **have used** rhino horns **for** short knives for centuries.

for는 기간(~동안)을 나타낼 때 쓰인다, 현재완료가 기간을 나타내는 전치사구와 쓰일 때에는 계속적 용법(~동안 계속 ...했다)의 의미를 가진다.

Review Test p.34

A

1 extinction 2 weapon
3 essential 4 defense
5 emphasize

B

1 ① 2 ③ 3 ①

C

1 Several of his paintings are nothing more than stripes on a canvas.

2 Whenever I attend the memorial service in my hometown, I miss him terribly.

3 Rich people have used rhino horns for short knives for centuries.

A

1 extinction: 멸종

2 weapon: 무기

3 essential: 중요한, 핵심적인

4 defense: 방어

5 emphasize: 강조하다

B

1 emerge: 나타나다(= appear)
보름달이 산 뒤에서 나타났다.

2 pass away: 돌아가시다(= die)
롭은 아버지가 돌아가시고 난 후 너무 우울해서 한 달 동안 집 밖에 나가지 않았다.

3 desire: 갈망하다(= long for)
이 자동차는 네가 원했던 모든 옵션을 가지고 있다.

C

1 nothing more than: ~에 지나지 않다, ~일 뿐이다

2 whenever+주어+동사: ~할 때마다

3 현재완료: have+p.p.
현재완료가 for와 같이 기간을 나타내는 전치사와 함께 쓰일 때 '계속'의 의미를 갖는다.

01 | PLACES p.37

1 ⑤ 2 ① 3 ①
4 merchant

마카오는 중화인민공화국의 특별행정구역이다. 마카오 반도는 홍콩의 서쪽에 있으며 작은 섬인 타이파와 콜로안을 포함한다. 마카오 문명은 6,000년이 넘게 지속하여 왔다.
(C) 그러나 16세기에 포르투갈 사람들이 마카오에 도착해서 마카오를 극동의 식민지로 삼았다. 상선들은 마카오를 다양한 상품을 위한 전초기지로 이용했다.
(B) 이 기지가 상인들로 하여금 중국과 서방 세계 사이에 중요한 무역관계를 시작할 수 있도록 하였다. 포르투갈 사람들은 오랫동안 마카오를 자국의 국외 영토로 간주했다.
(A) 하지만, 그들은 결국 마카오를 중화인민공화국에 반환하는 데 동의했다. 1999년 12월 20일, 포르투갈은 마카오 지배를 포기했다. 마카오는 현재 중국의 일부로 간주되고 있지만, 많은 정치적 문제에 있어서는 높은 수준의 자치권을 누리고 있다.

| 문제 해설 |

1 윗글은 마카오에 대한 역사적 사실을 시간의 흐름에 따라 설명한 것이다. (C) 포르투갈이 처음 마카오를 식민지로 삼게 된 내용 → (B) 포르투갈이 마카오를 식민지로 활용하는 내용 → (C) 포르투갈이 마카오를 중국에 반환하는 내용의 순서가 가장 적절하다.

2 ⓐ 마카오 반도가 타이파와 콜로안이라는 섬을 현재 포함하고 있다는 뜻이 되어야 하므로 included가 아니라 includes가 되어야 한다.

3 (a) as는 '~로서'라는 의미로 자격을 나타내는 전치사이다. ① ~로서 (전치사+명사(구)) ② ~처럼 (접속사+S+V) ③ ~와 같이 (as ~ as 비교) ④ ~ 때문에 (접속사+S+V) ⑤ ~함에 따라 (접속사+S+V)
① 그것을 칭찬으로 받아들일게.
② 너도 아는 것처럼, 나는 요즘에 꽤 바쁘다.
③ 그는 그 문제를 해결하려고 너만큼 열심히 노력했다.
④ 우리는 비가 그쳤기 때문에 영화를 보러 가기로 했다.
⑤ 시간에 지남에 따라 그는 교사가 한 말을 이해할 수 있게 되었다.

4 다른 나라와 물건을 사거나 파는 교역을 하는 사람은 상인(merchant)이다.

| 영영풀이 |

1 eventually: 마침내
2 colony: 식민지
3 province: (행정구역으로서의) 주(州)

| 구문풀이 |

5행 Its civilization **has existed** for over 6,000 years.
현재완료의 쓰임 중 계속을 의미한다.

12행 This post **allowed** merchants to open important trade relations **between** China **and** the Western world.
allow는 목적격 보어로 to부정사를 취하는 동사이며, 「allow+목적어+목적격 보어」는 '~가 …하는 것을 허락하다'라고 해석한다. 「between A and B」는 'A와 B 사이에'라는 뜻이다.

13행 The Portuguese **considered** Macau to be an overseas province for a long period of time.
「consider+목적어+목적격 보어」는 '~을 …라고 간주하다'라고 해석하며, 위 문장의 to be는 생략 가능하다.

02 | TRAGEDY p.39

1 ① 2 (A) was killed (B) killed
3 ④ 4 passenger

2001년 9월 11일에 미국에 어떤 일이 일어났는지 알고 있는가? 네 대의 항공기가 테러리스트에 의해 피랍되었고, 그중 두 대는 뉴욕에 있는 세계무역센터인 쌍둥이 빌딩에 부딪쳤다. 그 두 대의 항공기에 탑승한 사람들은 모두 죽었다. 또 다른 세 번째 비행기는 펜타곤(미국 국방부 건물)에 추락했다. 네 번째 비행기에 있던 몇몇 용감한 승객들이 펜실베니아 주의 한 들판에 추락하기 전에 비행기 탈주범들을 가까스로 제압했다.
그날 그 사건이 일어나자 모든 사람이 텔레비전 화면에 열중했다. 오사마 빈 라덴이 이 공격을 명령한 인물로 규명되었다. 곧이어 조지 W. 부시 미국 대통령이 테러와의 전쟁을 선포했다. 실제로 이 자살 공격은 거의 3천 명의 무고한 사람을 죽였다. 중동 출신의 종교적 광신도였던 열아홉 명의 비행기 납치범들도 전부 죽었다. 이 비극이 일어난 이후 미국인들은 어마어마한 분노와 슬픔을 느꼈다.
이를 추모하기 위한 노력으로 그들은 쌍둥이 빌딩이 서 있었던 같은 자리에 새로운 건물을 짓기 시작했고 2014년에 그 건물을 개관했다. 104층의 그 새로운 건물은 이제 '원 월드 무역센터'라고 불리며 미국인뿐만 아니라 전 세계의 평화를 사랑하는 사람들에게 희망과 승리의 상징이 되었다.

| 문제 해설 |

1 윗글은 2001년 9월 11일 일어났던 테러리스트의 잔인한 공격에 대해 전반적으로 다루고 있다.

윗글의 제목으로 가장 적절한 것은?

① 9월 11일에 발생한 잔인한 공격

② 쌍둥이 빌딩을 파괴한 사람

③ 9월 11일에 살아남은 사람들

④ 미국에서 발생한 테러와의 전쟁

⑤ 세계무역센터의 재건설

2 (A) 모든 승객이 죽임을 당하는 것이므로 수동형

(B) 이 자살 공격이 무고한 사람들을 죽인 것이므로 능동형

3 비행기 납치범의 세계무역센터 공격이 텔레비전으로 중계되었다.

① 네 대의 비행기가 세계무역센터에 충돌했다.

② 네 번째 비행기의 승객은 비행기 납치범에 의해 살해당했다.

③ 그 공격 이후에 비행기 납치범 중 몇 명이 붙잡혔다.

④ 많은 사람이 세계무역센터가 비행기 납치범에 의해 공격을 받는 것을 텔레비전으로 지켜보았다.

⑤ 비행기에 있던 탈주범 중 한 명은 오사마 빈 라덴이다.

4 운전자가 아니면서 자동차나 비행기, 기차 등을 타고 여행하는 사람은 승객(passenger)이다.

| 영영풀이 |

1 incident: 사고

2 suicide: 자살

3 tragedy: 비극

| 구문풀이 |

1행 Do you know **what** **happened** in the United States on September 11, 2001?

(what: S, happened: V)

간접의문문에서 종속절로 들어간 의문문은 「의문사+주어+동사」의 어순이지만, 의문사가 주어인 경우는 「의문사+동사」의 어순으로 쓴다.

5행 **Every** *passenger* on board the two airplanes **was killed**.

Every는 '모든'이라는 뜻으로 단수명사를 수식하고 단수동사로 받는다.

9행 everyone was glued to their television screens **as** the incidents took place

as는 '~ 하자마자, ~할 때'라는 의미로 시간 부사절을 이끄는 접속사이다.

10행 Osama Bin Laden was identified as *the man* **who** ordered these attacks.

be identified as: ~로 밝혀지다, 확인되다

who 이하는 주격 관계대명사절로 선행사 the man을 수식한다.

03 | INTERESTING FACTS p.41

1 ① 2 ⑤ 3 ② 4 methane

소는 매일 약 280 리터 가량의 메탄을 트림으로 방출한다. 이것은 그리 중요한 사실처럼 보이지 않으나, 소가 트림하면서 내는 메탄은 우리 환경에 위험한 요소이다. 메탄은 온실가스이고, 지구온난화는 이 온실가스와 연관이 있다. 미국 한 곳만 봐도, 매해 소에서 배출되는 6백만 톤의 메탄이 하늘로 올라간다. 전 세계적으로, 양, 염소, 들소를 포함하면 이 메탄 수치는 8천만 톤에 육박한다. 이산화탄소가 주요한 온실가스이나, 메탄은 대기 중의 열을 붙드는 데 있어 이산화탄소보다 21배나 더 효과적이다.

결론: 소가 트림을 할 때마다, 지구온난화와 극지방의 만년설을 녹이는 데 일조한다.

| 문제 해설 |

1 선행사(methane)가 이미 있으므로 관계대명사 what은 쓸 수 없다. what → that

2 belch(= burp): 트림하다

① 냄새 나다

② 표류하다

③ 가두다

④ 기여하다

⑤ 트림하다

3 A cow burps about 280 liters of methane every day.를 통해 소의 트림이 이산화탄소(carbon dioxide)가 아닌 메탄(methane)의 수치를 높인다는 것을 알 수 있다.

① 메탄은 온실가스다.

② 소가 트림하면 이산화탄소가 증가한다.

③ 지구온난화는 온실가스와 관계가 있다.

④ 메탄은 대기에서 열을 붙드는 데 매우 효과가 있다.

⑤ 미국에서 소는 매년 6백만 톤의 메탄을 생산해낸다.

4 소가 트림을 할 때 뱉어내는 메탄은 우리의 환경에 위험하다. 다른 가축들과 함께 소는 매일 메탄을 트림하면서 뱉어내고 이는 부정적인 방식으로 지구의 대기 온난화에 영향을 미친다.

| 영영풀이 |

1 burp/belch: 트림하다

2 trap: (흐름을) 막다, 잡다

3 contribute: 기여하다

| 구문풀이 |

7행 methane is **21 times more effective** at trapping heat in the atmosphere

「A is twice[three times]+비교급+than B」는 'A는 B보다 2배[3배] 더 ~하다'로 쓰이는 배수사 비교급 표현이다. 이 문장 뒤에는 than carbon dioxide가 생략되어있다.

9행 **Every time** a cow belches, it is contributing to global warming and the melting of the polar ice caps.
every time+주어+동사: ~할 때마다
every time은 시간부사절을 이끈다.

Review Test p.42

A
1 contribute 2 tragedy
3 colony 4 incident
5 eventually

B
1 ① 2 ③ 3 ⑤

C
1 The Portuguese considered Macau to be an overseas province for a long period of time.
2 Osama Bin Laden was identified as the man who ordered these attacks.
3 The methane that cows burp up is dangerous for our environment.

A

1 contribute: 기여하다
2 tragedy: 비극
3 colony: 식민지
4 incident: 사고
5 eventually: 마침내

B

1 relinquish: 포기하다(= give up)
그는 의장직을 포기하라는 압력을 받았다.
2 declare: 선언하다(= announce)
정부는 약물과 범죄와의 전쟁을 선포했다.
3 major: 주요한(= main)
테러리스트들은 유럽의 주요 도시 10군데 이상을 공격했다.

C

1 consider A (to be) B: A를 B라고 여기다
2 identify A as B: A를 B로 확인하다
(수동태: A is identified as B)
3 The methane: 선행사, that cows burp up: 목적격 관계대명사절

Unit 05

01 | CAMPAIGN p.45

1 ⑤ 2 ③ 3 ①
4 to complain

당신은 삶에서 얼마나 자주 문제점에 대해 불평하는가?
(C) 당신이 대부분의 사람과 마찬가지라면, 아마도 당신은 매일 문제점에 대해 불평할 것이다. 많은 사람이 문제를 고치려고 노력하는 것보다 불평하는 게 더 쉽다는 것을 안다. 이 말이 당신을 두고 하는 말처럼 들리는가? 그렇다면 당신은 '불평 없는 세상 프로젝트'(Complaint-Free World Project)에 대해 좀 알아 볼 필요가 있다.
(B) 그것은 매우 간단한 생각이고, 당신의 인생을 바꿔 줄 수도 있다! 몇몇 연구원은 나쁜 습관을 없애는 데 21일이 걸린다고 믿는다. 이 프로젝트를 시작하려면 오른쪽 손목에 자주색 팔찌를 차라. 당신의 목표는 스무하루 동안 같은 손목에 (계속) 팔찌를 차고 있는 것이다.
(A) 하지만, 당신이 누군가에 대해 불평이나, 험담, 비난을 하게 되면 팔찌를 다른 쪽 손목으로 옮기고, 모든 것을 다시 시작해야 한다. 그러니 불평을 중단하라! 당신 자신에 대해 기분이 훨씬 나아질 것이다.

| 문제 해설 |

1 윗글은 '불평 없는 세상 프로젝트'를 소개하고, 이 프로젝트의 실행 방법을 설명한 글이다. (C) '불평 제로 프로젝트'를 소개하기 위한 도입부 → (B) '불평 없는 세상 프로젝트'에 대한 설명 부분 → (A) '불평 없는 세상 프로젝트'를 통해 불평 없는 사회를 만들자는 내용으로 이어지는 것이 가장 적절하다.
2 한쪽 팔에 팔찌를 계속 차고 있다는 것은 불평하지 않았다는 뜻이므로 나쁜 습관을 없애는 데 21일이 걸린다는 내용이 가장 적절하다.
① 불평거리를 찾아내는 데
② 누군가를 비판하는 데
③ 나쁜 습관을 제거하는 데
④ 팔찌를 바꾸는 데
⑤ 자주색 팔찌를 받는 데
3 불평을 없애서 긍정적인 삶을 살자는 내용이다.
팔찌를 차는 목적은 쓸데없는 불평을 제거함으로써 우리의 삶에 긍정적인 변화를 가져오는 것이다.
① 긍정적인 … 제거함
② 부정적인 … 추가함
③ 긍정적인 … 비판함
④ 부정적인 … 감소시킴
⑤ 극적인 … 시작함

4 it은 가목적어로 진목적어는 to complain이다. 「주어+동사+목적어+목적격 보어」 구조에서 목적어가 to부정사면 목적어를 문장의 맨 뒤로 보내고 목적어 자리에 가목적어 it을 쓴다.

| 영영풀이 |

1 complain: 불평하다, 항의하다
2 gossip: 험담하다
3 daily: 매일

| 구문풀이 |

3행 if you complain, gossip about, or criticize **someone**, then you **must** move the bracelet onto your other wrist and start all over again
「complain (about someone), gossip about (someone), or criticize someone」의 구조로 이해하면 된다. move와 start는 must에 병렬 연결된 구조이다.

9행 Your goal is **to be wearing** it on the same wrist for twenty-one days.
21일 동안 팔찌를 차고 있는 것이므로 to부정사의 진행형이 쓰였다.

12행 If you're **like** most people, ~
여기서 like는 동사로 '~을 좋다하다'가 아닌 다른 도사와 함께 쓰여 전치사인 '~와 같은'의 의미로 쓰였다.

02 | FUTURE LIFE p.47

1 ① 2 ④ 3 ⑤
4 Space Tourism 또는 Space Travel

1969년에 인간이 최초로 달에 착륙한 이후 사람들은 우주여행이 어떻게 우리의 삶을 바꿀 수 있을지 궁금해 하기 시작했다. 사람이 달에서 살 수 있을까? 일반인이 우주를 여행할 수 있는 날은 언제일까? 글쎄, 아직은 아무도 달에 살지 않는다. 그러나 사람들은 드디어 우주여행을 하기 시작했다. 우주여행 산업은 매우 급격한 속도로 성장하고 있는 새로운 현상이다. 우주여행 산업은 사람들에게 우주로 여행할 기회를 준다. 불행하게도 그러한 기회는 당장은 아주 비싸다. 승객으로 우주선을 타고 우주여행을 하는 비용은 거의 3천5백만 달러이다. (마찬가지로 유람선 여행 비용은 급격히 올랐다.) 하지만, 일부 회사들은 덜 비싼 가격으로 관광객을 우주로 보낼 수 있는 우주선 개발에 착수하고 싶어 한다. 새로운 우주정거장이 건설 중이다. 심지어 우주에 호텔을 지으려는 계획도 있다! 불행하게도, 일반인이 별에서 휴가를 보낼 수 있기까지는 여전히 오랜 시간이 걸릴 것 같다.

| 문제 해설 |

1 두 개의 빈칸 뒤에 모두 부정적인 내용이 나오므로 Unfortunately가 가장 적절하다.
① 불행하게도
② 마침내
③ 다행히도
④ 곧
⑤ 갑자기

2 윗글은 우주선 여행에 관한 글로 ⓓ의 유람선 여행 비용에 관한 문장은 흐름과 관계없다.

3 평범한 사람들이 우주여행을 하려면 오랜 시간이 걸릴 거라고 했으므로 일치하지 않는 것은 ⑤번이다.
① 사람은 이미 달을 방문했었다.
② 새 우주 정거장이 건설 중이다.
③ 우주여행 비용은 엄청나게 비싸다.
④ 사람들은 장차 우주의 호텔에서 머물 수 있을지도 모른다.
⑤ 머지않아 평범한 사람들이 우주여행을 할 수 있게 될 것이다.

4 윗글의 전반적인 내용은 우주여행에 관한 것이므로 제목이 될 수 있는 말은 Space Tourism이나 Space Travel이다.

| 영영풀이 |

1 phenomenon: 현상
2 opportunity: 기회
3 attempt: 시도

| 구문풀이 |

2행 people began to wonder **how** space travel would change our lives
(의문사: how, 주어: space travel, 동사: would change)
의문사 how는 wonder의 목적어절을 이끈다.

6행 Space tourism is *a new phenomenon* **which** is growing very quickly.
which는 선행사 a new phenomenon을 수식하는 주격 관계대명사절을 이끌고 있다.

8행 The cost of traveling into space as a passenger on a spaceship is almost thirty-five million dollars.
The cost가 주어, is가 동사이다.

10행 some companies want to start creating *spaceships* **that** can take tourists into space **less expensively**
that 이하는 선행사 spaceships를 수식하는 주격 관계대명사절이다. 「less+부사」는 비교급 표현으로 '덜 ~하게'라고 해석한다.

12행 New space stations **are being built.**
are being built는 현재진행 수동으로 New space stations가 지어지는 것이고, 현재 진행되고 있음을 나타낸다.

12행 **There have** even **been** *attempts* to begin **building** a hotel in space!
there are[is]는 '~이 있다'라는 뜻이고, there have been은 과거의 어느 시점부터 지금까지 계속 존재해 왔던 것을 뜻한다. begin은 to부정사나 동명사를 목적어로 취할 수 있는데 여기서는 building이라는 동명사를 목적어로 취했다. 「to begin ~ in space」가 attempts를 뒤에서 수식하고 있다.

03 | WORLD NEWS

p.49

1 ② 2 ② 3 ②
4 endangered

(B) 전 세계에는 약 6,800개의 언어가 있다. 그러나 그 중에서 거의 절반에 해당되는 언어가 그 언어를 사용하는 문화가 소멸되면서 같이 사라지고 있다. 이 멸종 위기한 처한 언어들은 무엇이며 왜 그것들은 사라질까?
(A) 멸종 위기에 처한 언어란 그 언어만을 사용하는 사람이 거의 없게 된 언어를 말한다. 멸종 위기에 처한 언어는 멸종 위기에 처한 소수 문화의 언어이다. 문화를 다음 세대로 제일 잘 전하는 수단은 언어이기 때문에, 언어가 사라지면 그 문화도 사라진다. 슬프게도, 수천 개의 언어가 사라졌으며, 지금은 그 사라지는 속도가 더 빨라지고 있다. 전 세계의 언어 중에서 약 50%가 멸종 위기에 직면하고 있는 것이다. 그 가운데 90%가 아마도 한 달에 두 개 꼴로 사라질 것이라고 우려하는 학자들이 많다.
(C) 언어가 사라지는 원인에는 어떤 것들이 있을까? 도시의 성장, 전 세계적인 통신망의 발달, 서구화, 인종 차별, 기아 등의 원인을 들 수 있을 것이다. 이러한 이유 때문에 소수의 사회에 속한 사람들은 자신들의 언어를 다음 세대로 전파하는 것을 창피하게 생각한다. 또한 다수가 사용하는 언어를 말하는 어린이가 미래에 성공할 가능성이 더 많다고 생각하는 사람들이 많다.

| 문제 해설 |

1 (B) 멸종 위기에 처한 언어들에 대해 문제 제기 → (A) 멸종 위기에 처한 언어의 정의 설명 → (C) 언어가 사라지는 원인 설명

2 Reasons such as these: the growth of cities, worldwide communication, Westernization, discrimination, starvation, and so on을 통해 도시의 성장, 전 세계적인 통신망의 발달, 서구화, 인종 차별, 기아 등이 언어를 사라지게 하는 원인으로 언급되었다. ②의 '고어의 어려움'은 언급되지 않았다.
① 차별
② 고어의 어려움
③ 서구화
④ 굶주림
⑤ 도시의 성장

3 About 50% of the world's languages face extinction을 통해 세계 언어의 반 정도가 멸종 위기에 직면하고 있음을 알 수 있다.
① 1/4
② 절반
③ 대부분
④ 6,800개
⑤ 2개

4 멸종 위기 언어는 가까운 미래에 멸종될 가능성이 있는 언어이다. 그것은 멸종 위기에 처한 소수 문화가 사용하는 언어이다. 언어가 소멸하는 몇 가지 이유에는 도시의 성장, 전 세계적인 통신망의 발달, 서구화, 차별, 기아 등이 있다.

| 영영풀이 |

1 generation: 세대
2 starvation: 기아, 굶주림
3 ashamed: 부끄러운, 수치스러운

| 구문풀이 |

2행 An **endangered** language is a language with nearly no one who speaks only that language.
동사 endanger(~을 위험에 처하게 하다)가 과거분사 형태로 language를 수식하고 있다. language는 위험에 처해지는 대상이므로 수동관계에 있으므로 과거분사 형태로 쓰였다.

4행 Cultures are best passed on to **following** generations through their languages,
동사 follow(뒤따르다)가 현재분사 형태로 generations를 수식하고 있다. generations는 앞선 세대를 뒤따르는 주체이므로 능동관계에 있으므로 현재분사 형태로 쓰였다.

16행 These **make** people who belong to small communities **feel ashamed to pass on their languages.**
make는 동사원형을 목적격 보어로 취하는 사역동사이다. people이 목적격 보어, feel ashamed 이하가 목적격 보어이다. who belong to small communities는 people을 수식하는 관계대명사절이다.

Review Test p.50

A

1 starvation　2 opportunity
3 generation　4 attempt
5 complain

B

1 ③　2 ⑤　3 ⑤

C

1 A lot of people find it easier to complain than try to fix them.
2 Some companies want to start creating spaceships that can take tourists into space less expensively.
3 These make people who belong to small communities feel ashamed to pass on their languages.

A

1 starvation: 기아, 굶주림
2 opportunity: 기회
3 generation: 세대
4 attempt: 시도
5 complain: 불평하다, 항의하다

B

1 gossip: 험담하다, 소문을 퍼뜨리다(= spread rumors)
아무도 베키와 친구가 되고 싶지 않는 이유는 그녀가 다른 사람들을 험담하기 때문이다.
2 average: 보통의(= common)
보통 사람들은 매일 물을 얼마나 많이 마시나요?
3 rate: 속도(= speed)
한국의 경제 성장률은 내년에 줄어들 가능성이 있다.

C

1 find it easy[difficult, boring etc.] to부정사: ~하는 것이 쉽다[어렵다, 지루하다 ...]고 생각하다
(it: 가목적어, to부정사: 진목적어)
2 want to부정사: ~하기를 원하다
start+to부정사/동명사: ~하기를 시작하다
3 make: 5형식 동사
people who belong to small communities: 목적어
feel ashamed to pass on their languages: 목적격 보어

01 | FESTIVALS p.53

1 ②　2 ⑤　3 ④
4 조각을 적절하게 디자인할 수 있는 충분한 능력(전기톱이나 조각칼 같은 다양한 도구를 사용할 줄 아는 능력)

전 세계 각국에서 많은 겨울 축제가 열린다. 하지만, 일본의 삿포로 눈축제만큼 인상적인 축제는 거의 없다. 2월에 이레 동안 도시는 수백 개의 아름다운 눈 동상과 얼음 조각으로 장식된다. 예술가들은 수많은 다양한 조각상을 전시하려고 모여든다. 이들 조각품은 유명한 건물, 사람, 역사적 사건을 표현한다. 그들은 조각품을 제대로 디자인할 수 있는 상당한 기술을 지니고 있어야 한다. 그들은 전기톱과 작은 끌 같은 다양한 도구를 사용하는 방법을 알아야 한다. 밤에는 얼음 조각품이 반짝이는 색색의 조명을 받아 빛이 난다. 축제에는 음악 공연과 맛있는 음식도 있다. 해산물과 감자, 옥수수, 신선한 유제품을 맛볼 수 있다. 매년 미인대회도 열린다. 우승자는 스스키노 얼음의 여왕으로 선포된다. 매년 약 300개의 조각품이 만들어지고, 이 독특한 축제를 즐기기 위해 2백만 명이 삿포로를 방문한다.

| 문제 해설 |

1 빈칸 (A)의 앞뒤에서 상반된 내용이 나오므로 빈칸 (A)에는 However가 와야 한다. 빈칸 (C) 뒤에서 a variety of tools의 예를 들고 있으므로 빈칸 (C)에는 such as가 와야 한다.
① 게다가 … ~와 달리
② 하지만 … ~와 같은
③ ~에도 불구하고 … ~와 같은
④ 그러므로 … ~뿐만 아니라
⑤ 다시 말해서 … ~뿐만 아니라
2 These는 앞에 나온 a huge variety of sculptures를 가리킨다.
(B) These가 가리키는 것은 무엇인가?
① 도구들
② 예술가들
③ 축제들
④ 국가들
⑤ 조각들
3 주어진 문장에서 음식을 먹을 수 있다는 이야기가 나오므로 delicious food라는 문구가 나온 뒤인 ⓓ에 들어가는 것이 가장 적절하다.
해산물과 감자, 옥수수, 신선한 유제품들을 맛볼 수 있다.
4 They must possess a great deal of skill to design their sculptures properly.에서 예술가들이 갖춰야 할 능력을 알 수 있다.

| 영영풀이 |

1 possess: 소유하다
2 illuminate: ~을 밝게 비추다
3 distinctive: 눈에 띄는, 특이한

| 구문풀이 |

2행 **few** of them are **as** impressive **as** the Sapporo Snow Festival in Japan
few는 수량형용사로 거의 없음을 의미할 때 사용하고 약간 있음을 의미할 때는 a few를 사용한다. 「as+형용사/부사 원급+as」는 두 대상을 비교할 때 쓰는 구문으로 '~만큼 …하다'라고 해석한다. 여기에서는 이 표현이 few와 함께 쓰여 최상급을 의미한다.

6행 They must possess **a great deal of** *skill* to design their sculptures properly.
a great deal of는 '많은'이라는 의미로, 셀 수 없는 명사를 수식한다. skill은 to부정사가 이끄는 구의 수식은 받는다.

7행 They must know **how to use** a variety of tools ~.
how to+동사원형: ~하는 방법

10행 There is even *a beauty contest* **held** each year.
held each year가 a beauty contest를 수식하고, contest와 held 사이에 which is가 생략되었다고 생각하면 이해하기 쉽다.

02 | PEOPLE p.55

1 ③ 2 ①
3 a communist picture of Lenin on the RCA Building at the Rockefeller Center in Manhattan

프레스코 벽화는 회반죽이 아직 젖어 있는 동안 벽에 그려지는 그림이다. 유럽에서 르네상스 시기에 이러한 기법이 널리 유행했고, 많은 화가가 건물과 교회의 돔형 천장을 장식하기 위해 이 기법을 사용했다. 가장 유명한 프레스코 화가 중 한 사람은 디에고 리베라였다. 그는 멕시코에서 이러한 미술 형식의 부활이 일어나게 했다. 1886년에 태어난 디에고는 멕시코에서 미술을 공부했다. 그는 1907년에 그림 공부를 계속하려고 유럽으로 떠났다. 그가 멕시코로 돌아오자 정부는 그의 작업을 후원하는 데 동의했다. 그는 멕시코 역사를 묘사한 수많은 벽화를 그렸다. 디에고 리베라는 미국에서도 활동했다. 그는 샌프란시스코 주식거래소 시티 클럽과 캘리포니아 미술 학교를 위한 벽화를 그렸다. 그리고 한번은 맨해튼 록펠러 센터에 있는 RCA 건물에 레닌의 공산주의적 그림을 그렸다. 이는 그 예술가에 대한 큰 논쟁을 불러일으켰으며 그의 벽화는 곧이어 파괴되었다. 그의 작품이 모두에게 환영 받은 것은 아니었지만, 그는 미국의 대중예술에 영향을 주었다. 리베라는 1957년, 70세의 나이로 멕시코시티에서 사망했다. 오늘날까지도 그는 여전히 멕시코의 가장 사랑 받는 화가 중 한 명이다.

| 문제 해설 |

1 윗글은 벽화가 디에고 리베라의 작품과 삶에 관한 이야기이다.
윗글의 제목으로 가장 적절한 것은?
① 멕시코에 있는 리베라의 벽화
② 프레스코 벽화의 정의
③ 디에고 리베라의 작품과 삶
④ 프레스코 벽화를 그리는 사람들
⑤ 르네상스 시대의 이탈리아 벽화가인 디에고 리베라

2 (A) one이 주어이므로 was가 와야 한다. (B) 「agree+to+동사원형」이므로 sponsor가 와야 한다. (C) 그의 작품이 환영 받지 못하는 것이므로 수동형인 welcomed가 와야 한다.

3 파괴된 그의 벽화는 맨해튼에 있는 록펠러 센터에 그려진 레닌의 그림이다.

| 영영풀이 |

1 depict: ~을 그리다, 묘사하다
2 mural: 벽화
3 controversy: 논쟁

| 구문풀이 |

1행 Fresco painting is *a picture* **that** is painted on a wall while the plaster is still wet.
that 이하는 주격 관계대명사절로 선행사 a picture를 수식한다.

7행 **Born in 1886,** Diego studied art in Mexico.
Born in 1886은 분사구문으로 Diego was born in 1886 and he studied art in Mexico.정도로 바꿔 쓸 수 있다.

9행 He painted ***a number of*** *murals* **that** depict scenes from Mexican history.
a number of는 '많은'이라는 뜻으로 셀 수 있는 명사를 수식한다. that 이하는 주격 관계대명사절로 선행사 a number of murals를 수식한다.

03 | SOCIAL ISSUES p.57

1 ④ 2 ② 3 ③
4 smoking, curious

여러분 안녕하세요. 저는 보건복지부의 이 박사입니다. 오늘은 한국의 십 대들의 흡연관련 설문 조사에 대해서 이야기를 나누려고 합니다. 저희는 십 대 흡연자의 수가 심각할 정도로 늘어났다는 것을 파악했습니다. 십 대들이 흡연을 시작하게 되는 주된 동기와 청소년 흡연문제가 왜 심각한지, 그리고 어떤 조치를 취해야 할 지에 대해서 보고 드리겠습니다.
먼저 친구들이 십 대들에게 미치는 영향은 큽니다. 이런 일을 '동료 압력'이라고 하는데 이런 부담감이 십 대들이 흡연을 시작하는 이유가 될 수 있습니다. 두 번째로 (a) 그들(= 십 대들)은 단지 흡연에 대한 호기심으로 시작하기도 합니다. 또한, 유명인에게도 영향을 받습니다. 십 대들은 보통 그들이 좋아하는 배우나 가수들처럼 행동하고 싶어 하고 (b) 그들(= 배우나 가수들)이 흡연하는 모습을 멋있다고 생각하는 거죠.

그렇다면 십 대의 흡연이 왜 이렇게 심각한 걱정거리일까요? 흡연을 일찍 시작할수록 니코틴 중독에서 벗어나는 것이 더욱 어렵다는 것이 연구에서 나타났습니다. 불행하게도 통상적으로 흡연을 하는 십 대들의 경우 세 명 중의 한 명이 흡연으로 인해 일찍 죽을 것이고, 흡연하는 십 대 중 절반이 담배 관련 병에 걸려 죽을 것입니다.

| 문제 해설 |

1 (A) 두 번째로 십 대들은 흡연하기 시작하는데 보통 그들(= 십 대들)이 그것에 관해 호기심이 있어서이다. (B) 그들은 대개 자신이 좋아하는 배우나 가수들처럼 행동하길 원하고, 십 대들은 그들이 흡연하는 것을 볼 때 그들(= 배우나 가수들)이 멋있어 보인다고 생각한다.

2 글의 도입부에서 십 대들의 흡연 동기, 십 대 흡연 문제가 심각한 이유, 십 대 흡연을 해결하기 위한 방법 순으로 글이 전개될 것이라고 했다. 이어지는 두 번째, 세 번째 단락에서 십 대가 흡연을 시작하는 이유와 십 대 흡연이 심각한 이유가 각각 제시되고 있으므로 뒤에 이어질 내용으로 해결 방법이 나와야 자연스럽다.

① 흡연 관련 질병 목록

② 십 대 흡연을 어떻게 줄일 것인가

③ 한국에서 얼마나 많은 유명인들이 흡연하는가

④ 흡연 청소년과의 인터뷰

⑤ 건강 전문가들이 10대 흡연에 대해 얼마나 걱정하는가

3 the earlier a teen begins smoking, the more difficult it is to break the nicotine addiction을 통해 흡연을 일찍 시작할수록 니코틴 중독에서 벗어나는 것이 더 어렵다는 것을 알 수 있다. 따라서 ③은 글의 내용과 일치하지 않는다.

① 한국에서 흡연하는 십 대가 늘어났다.

② 어떤 십 대는 호기심 때문에 흡연을 시작한다.

③ 십 대가 흡연을 일찍 시작할수록, 금연하기 쉬워진다.

④ 친구가 당신의 결정에 영향을 미치는 것을 동료 압력이라 한다.

⑤ 십 대 흡연자의 절반은 흡연 관련 질병으로 사망할 것이다.

4 한국 십 대들은 친구에게 영향을 받아서, 스타들처럼 되고 싶어서, 아니면 단지 <u>호기심</u> 때문에 <u>흡연</u>을 시작한다. 흡연은 이득이 없는 나쁜 습관이다.

| 영영풀이 |

1 motivation: 자극, 동기

2 curious: 호기심 있는

3 addiction: 중독

| 구문풀이 |

11행 when they **see** them **smoking**, teenagers think they look cool

see와 같은 지각동사는 동사원형이나 현재분사를 목적격 보어로 취할 수 있다. 「see+목적어+동사원형/현재분사」는 '~가 …하는 것을 보다'라는 의미를 가진다.

14행 **the earlier** a teen begins smoking, **the more difficult** it is to break the nicotine addiction

「the 비교급 ~, the 비교급 …」은 '~하면 할수록 더 …하다'라는 의미를 가지는 표현이다. 이 문장에서 it은 가주어, to break 이하는 진주어이다.

Review Test

p.58

A

1 addiction
2 controversy
3 motivation
4 distinctive
5 possess

B

1 ⑤
2 ②
3 ④

C

1 They must know how to use a variety of tools such as chain saws and small chisels.
2 He painted a number of murals that depict scenes from Mexican history.
3 The earlier a teen begins smoking, the more difficult it is to break the nicotine addiction.

A

1 addiction: 중독
2 controversy: 논쟁
3 motivation: 자극, 동기
4 distinctive: 눈에 띄는, 특이한
5 possess: 소유하다

B

1 display: 전시하다(= exhibit)
국립박물관은 몇몇 현대 미술가의 작품을 전시할 것이다.

2 inspire: 영감을 주다, 자극하다(= stimulate)
그녀의 강연은 정말 우리가 환경을 보호하도록 자극했다.

3 behave: 행동하다(= act)
성인 팬들 몇 명은 야구장에서 어린아이처럼 행동했다.

C

1 how to부정사: ~하는 방법

2 a number of murals: 선행사
that depict scenes from Mexican history: 주격 관계대명사절

3 the 비교급, the 비교급: ~하면 할수록 더 …하다

01 | HISTORY p.61

1 ②　　2 ④　　3 ⑤

프랑스혁명은 1789년에 시작되어 이후 약 10년간 계속되었고, 서양사의 중요한 사건이었다. 궁극적으로 이 혁명은 프랑스에서 군주제 몰락의 원인이 되었다. 몇 가지 요소가 프랑스혁명에 기여했다. 혁명이 있기 전에 유럽에서 삶의 질은 가족의 신분에 따라 결정되었다. 누군가 가난한 가정에 태어났다면 그의 일생도 가난했다. 가난하다면 신분을 상승시키는 것은 불가능했다. 불공정한 세법은 가난한 사람들이 돈을 많이 가질 수 없는 상태로 만들었다. 심각한 식량 부족 사태 역시 소작인에게 수많은 고난을 야기했다. 반면에 부자는 편안한 삶을 누렸으며, 군주 일가는 소작농들의 운명에는 관심이 없어 보였다. 소작인은 부유한 귀족에게 매우 분노하게 되었다. 그들은 프랑스 사회에서 더 많은 평등을 원했고, 1789년에 마침내 프랑스의 정치적 풍경을 바꾸어 놓고, 프랑스 국민에게 정치적 힘을 준 폭력적인 정치적 혁명이 시작되었다.

| 문제 해설 |

1 이 글은 프랑스혁명이 일어나게 된 원인과 그 결과에 대한 이야기이다.

① 프랑스에서 신분을 상승시키는 방법
② 프랑스혁명의 원인과 결과
③ 프랑스혁명이 실패한 이유
④ 시골에 사는 프랑스 소작농의 삶
⑤ 프랑스혁명이 서양사에 끼친 영향

2 ⓐ It은 to raise your status를 받는 가주어이다. ①번 대명사, ②번 대명사, ③번 It ~ that 강조 구문의 it, ④번 to translate Korean into English를 받는 가주어, ⑤번 비인칭 주어(날씨)이다.

① 그것이 너무 지루해서 나는 잠이 들었다.
② 그것은 내 것은 아니지만, 네가 그것을 사용해도 돼.
③ 저 아름다운 사진을 찍은 사람은 바로 헨리였다.
④ 한국어를 영어로 번역하는 것은 어렵다.
⑤ 밖에는 여전히 비가 내리니까 집에 머무는 것이 낫겠다.

3 왕의 폭력적인 군림에 대한 언급은 없다.

| 영영풀이 |

1 revolution: 혁명
2 shortage: 부족
3 resentful: 분개한

| 구문풀이 |

1행 *The French Revolution*, **which** began in 1789 and lasted for about ten years, was an important event in Western history.
which는 The French Revolution을 선행사로 받는 계속적 용법의 주격 관계대명사이다.

7행 **If** you were born into a poor family, your life would be one of poverty.
If는 조건 부사절을 이끄는 종속접속사이다. 가난하게 태어났다면 그 사람의 삶도 가난했다는 의미이다. you는 '너'라는 특정인이 아니라 일반적인 사람을 가리킨다.

13행 they finally launched *a violent political revolution* **which** changed France's political landscape and ~.
which가 이끄는 주격 관계대명사절은 선행사 a violent political revolution을 수식한다.

02 | ANIMALS p.63

1 ⑤　　2 ④　　3 ②　　4 habitat

거대한 털매머드를 직접 마주친 적이 있는가? 마주친 적이 있다면 그것은 박물관 안에서였을 것이다. 왜냐하면 이 거대한 짐승은 지금 멸종 상태이기 때문이다. 털매머드는 지구상에 살았던 가장 큰 생물 중 하나였다. 그것은 흔히 16피트 크기로 자랐고 6에서 8톤의 무게가 나갔다. 이 동물이 왜 지금은 지구를 배회하지 않는 것인가? 약 1만 년 전에 털매머드의 수가 줄어들기 시작했으며, 기원전 1,600년경에는 얼마 안 남았던 이 종의 표본들마저 죽어버리고 말았다. 많은 연구원들은 기후 변화가 중요한 원인이었다고 결론을 내렸다. 12,000년 전, 지구 온도가 올라가기 시작해서 전 세계의 빙하 지역이 녹기 시작했다. 이러한 현상은 "빙하 후퇴"라고 불리는데, 그것이 털매머드의 자연 서식지를 급격하게 감소시켰다. 매머드의 멸종에 기여한 또 다른 요소는 인간의 활동이었다. 진보된 인간 사냥꾼의 확산이 털매머드 멸종에 있어서 가장 주요한 원인이었던 듯하다. 실제로 과학자들은 털매머드를 사냥하는 사람들을 묘사한 동굴 벽화를 발견했다.

| 문제 해설 |

1 윗글은 털매머드가 멸종된 이유에 대해 설명한 글이다.
윗글의 제목으로 가장 적절한 것은?

① 박물관에서 볼 수 있는 동물들
② 빙하 후퇴가 일어난 이유
③ 털매머드를 볼 수 있는 장소
④ 털매머드의 자연 서식지 연구
⑤ 털매머드가 사라진 이유

2 인간의 사냥 활동이 털매머드의 멸종에 영향을 주었다는 문장의 앞인 ⓓ가 가장 적절한 곳이다.
털매머드의 멸종에 기여한 또 다른 요소는 인간의 활동이었다.

3 인간의 활동이 털매머드의 멸종에 영향을 주었다고 했으므로 털매머드를 사냥하는 사람의 그림이 있었다는 내용이 가장 적절하다.
① 털매머드를 기르는 사람들
② 털매머드를 사냥하는 사람들
③ 빙하 위에서 사는 털매머드
④ 털매머드의 자연 서식지
⑤ 털매머드와 놀고 있는 아이들

4 특정한 동물이 거주하거나, 식물이 자라는 곳은 habitat(서식지)이다.

| 영영풀이 |

1 roam: ~을 돌아다니다
2 specimen: 표본, 실례
3 drastically: 급격하게

| 구문풀이 |

1행 **Have you ever come** face-to-face with a giant wooly mammoth? If you **have**, then it **must have been** inside a museum because this magnificent beast is now extinct.
Have you ever come은 현재완료 중 경험을 묻는 표현이다. If you have는 If you have come face-to-face with a giant wooly mammoth를 줄여 쓴 것이다. 「must have p.p.」는 과거에 대한 강한 추측을 의미하는 조동사로 '~이었음이 틀림없다'라고 해석한다.

9행 Many researchers have concluded **that** climate change was a significant factor.
that은 have concluded의 목적어절을 이끄는 접속사로 생략할 수 있다.

14행 scientists have discovered *cave drawings* **that** illustrate *humans* **hunting** wooly mammoths
that은 주격 관계대명사로 선행사 cave drawings를 수식하는 절을 이끈다. hunting wooly mammoths가 humans를 뒤에서 수식한다.

03 | ENVIRONMENT p.65

1 ① 2 ③ 3 ②
4 The ozone layer, CFCs, halons

오존층에 구멍이 생긴 것을 처음 발견한 때는 1984년이다. 과학자들은 남극 상공의 오존양이 정상보다 적다는 것을 발견했던 것이다. 그 이후에 지구상의 다른 곳에서도 오존층에 구멍이 발견되었다. 왜 이것이 중요한가?
오존층은 태양에서 나오는 자외선으로부터 우리를 보호해 주기 때문에 중요하다. UV-B라고 부르는 이 자외선은 인간, 동물 및 식물에 유해하다. (매일 자외선 차단 크림을 바르는 것이 중요하다.) 그것은 암을 유발하기도 하고, 동물의 눈에 손상을 입히며, 또한 일부 식물의 성장률을 저해하기도 한다.
오존층의 구멍은 우리가 방출하는 어떤 기체 때문에 생긴다. 이 기체를 CFC라고 부른다. 이 기체는 냉장고, 차량의 냉방기, 에어로졸 등에 들어 있다. 소화기에 쓰이는 할론이라고 부르는 다른 기체도 오존층에 구멍을 만든다. 이 문제를 해결하는 유일한 방법은 CFC나 할론을 포함하고 있는 제품을 덜 사용하고, 덜 만드는 것밖에는 없다.

| 문제 해설 |

1 윗글은 오존층에 구멍이 생긴 것과 그 원인과 영향에 대해서 설명하는 글이다.
① 오존층의 구멍
② 오존층
③ 자외선
④ CFC
⑤ 할론

2 윗글의 오존층에 관한 글로서 오존층이 자외선을 차단하는 역할이 중요한 것이지 (C)의 '매일 자외선 차단 크림을 바르는 것이 중요하다.'는 글의 전체 흐름에 불필요하다.

3 The ozone layer is important because it protects us from the ultraviolet light that comes from the sun.을 통해 오존층은 태양에서 나오는 자외선으로부터 우리를 보호해 주기 때문에 중요하다는 것을 알 수 있다.
① 할론으로부터 우리를 보호한다.
② 자외선으로부터 우리를 보호한다.
③ CFC로부터 우리를 보호한다.
④ 지구 온난화를 야기한다.
⑤ 우리로 하여금 냉장고와 차량 냉방기를 이용할 수 있도록 한다.

4 오존층은 우리 환경에 매우 중요한데, 1984년 이래 전 세계적으로 오존층에 구멍이 생긴 것이 발견되었다. 이것은 인간, 동물, 식물에 심각한 문제를 일으킬 수 있다. 과학자들은 오존층을 보호하는 방법은 CFC나 할론 등 유해한 기체를 포함한 제품을 덜 사용하고, 덜 만드는 것밖에는 없다고 말한다.

| 영영풀이 |

1 reduce: 줄이다, 감소시키다
2 rate: 빈도, 발생률
3 release: 배출하다, 내놓다

| 구문풀이 |

12행 **Other gases** called halons that are used in fire extinguishers also **make** holes in the ozone layer.
이 문장의 주어는 Other gases, 동사는 make인데, 주어와 동사 사이에 수식어구가 있다. called halons(=that are called halons)는 Other gases를 수식하는 분사구, that are used in fire extinguishers는 바로 앞의 halons를 수식하는 관계대명사절이다.

13행 The only possible solution to the problem is **using and making less products that contain CFCs or halons.**
using and making 이하는 현재진행형을 만드는 현재분사가 아니라 주어 The only possible solution to the problem에 대한 보어 역할을 하는 동명사이다.

Review Test p.66

A

1 drastically 2 revolution
3 reduce 4 roam
5 resentful

B

1 ① 2 ③ 3 ②

C

1 The monarchy did not seem to care about the fate of the peasantry.
2 Another factor that contributed to the extinction of the wooly mammoth was human activity.
3 The holes in the ozone layer are caused by certain gases we release.

A

1 drastically: 급격하게
2 revolution: 혁명
3 reduce: 줄이다, 감소시키다
4 roam: ~을 돌아다니다
5 resentful: 분개한

B

1 unfair: 부당한(= unjust)
나는 부의 불공평한 분배가 가장 심각한 문제라고 생각한다.
2 inhabit: ~에서 살다, 거주하다(= dwell in)
많은 야생 동물들이 이 숲에서 산다. 우리는 숲을 개발하면 안 된다.
3 release: 배출하다(= emit)
화학반응이 일어나는 중에 배출되는 가스를 마시지 마세요.

C

1 seem to부정사: ~인 것 같다
2 contribute to: ~에 기여하다
3 The holes in the ozone layer: 주어
are caused: 동사(수동태)
by certain gases we release: by+행위자
(we release: certain gases를 수식하는 관계대명사절)

01 | ART p.69

1 ① 2 ④ 3 ②
4 I was accustomed to getting up early.

인상주의 예술작품은 19세기에 프랑스에서 시작되었다. 인상주의는 전통적인 예술작품에서 상당히 벗어나 있었다. 인상주의 이전의 예술작품은 대개 왕족 혹은 종교인을 묘사했으며, 그들은 주로 그림의 가운데에 배치되었다. 하지만, 그림의 배경은 중요시 하지 않았다. 인상주의의 도입은 예술이란 무엇인가와 예술작품이 어떻게 만들어지는가에 대한 오랜 믿음을 변화시켰다. 예술가들은 집 밖의 아름다운 경치를 묘사하는 데 초점을 맞추기 시작했다. 인상파 화가들은 흔히 풍경, 인물, 역사적 사건을 그렸다. 그들은 자연을 객관적으로 묘사하기 위해 직사광선뿐 아니라 반사광선도 사용했다. 이는 사람들 대부분이 익숙하게 보아왔던 것과는 사뭇 달랐다. 그림의 모든 부분이 중요했다. 더 나아가 그림에 묘사된 사람이 항상 왕족인 것은 아니었다. 누구든 그림의 대상이 될 수 있었다! 공원에서 걷고 있는 사람도, 술집의 바텐더도 그림의 대상이 될 수 있었다. 유명한 인상파 화가들로는 르누아르, 모네, 드가 등이 있다.

| 문제 해설 |

1 (A) 예술작품이 왕족이나 종교적인 인물을 묘사했다는 의미이므로 depicted가 적절하다. (B) from의 목적어가 되면서 seeing의 목적어도 되는 선행사를 포함한 관계대명사 what이 적절하다. (C) 사람이 공원을 걸어 다니는 것이므로 능동의 의미를 갖는 현재분사 walking이 적절하다.

2 공원을 걸어 다니는 사람처럼 평범한 사람도 그림의 대상이 될 수 있었다는 내용이므로 '누구나 그림의 대상이 될 수 있었다!'가 적절하다.
① 누구라도 그릴 수 있었다!
② 아무도 그릴 수 없었다!
③ 아무도 그림의 대상이 될 수 없었다!
④ 누구든 그림의 대상이 될 수 있었다!
⑤ 아무도 그림을 살 수 없었다!

3 인상주의 이전의 그림은 배경을 중요시하지 않았다.

4 '~하는 데 익숙하다'라는 표현은 「be accustomed to+(동)명사」이다.

| 영영풀이 |

1 departure: 이탈, 벗어남; 출발
2 figure: 인물
3 accustomed: 익숙해진

| 구문풀이 |

4행 artwork usually depicted *royalty or religious figures*, **who** were usually placed in the center of the painting
who는 선행사 royalty or religious figures를 받는 계속적 용법의 주격 관계대명사이고, and they로 바꿔 쓸 수 있다.

6행 The introduction of Impressionism changed the old belief **of** what art was **and** how artwork was created.
what art was와 how artwork was created가 of에 and로 병렬 연결된 구조이다.

10행 They used **not only** direct **but** reflected light *to depict* nature objectively.
「not only A but (also) B」는 'A뿐만 아니라 B도'라고 해석한다. to depict는 to부정사의 부사적 쓰임 중 목적을 의미하며 in order to[so as to]로 바꿔 쓸 수 있다.

12행 *the people* that were depicted in the paintings **were not always** from a royal family
that은 주격 관계대명사로 선행사 the people을 수식하는 절을 이끈다. were의 주어는 the people이다. 사람들이 그림에 묘사된 것이므로 수동태로 쓰였다. not always는 부분 부정을 의미하며 '항상 ~한 것은 아니다'라고 해석한다.

02 | SPECIAL DAYS p.71

1 ③ 2 ③ 3 ②
4 손님을 보호하려고

박싱데이는 연중 가장 쇼핑하기 좋은 날 중 하루이다. 이날은 크리스마스 바로 다음 날인 12월 26일이다. 박싱데이는 많은 상점이 연중 최고의 매상을 올린다. 상점은 종종 가장 많이 할인된 가격으로 상품을 판매한다. 이 점이 상당히 많은 사람을 유인한다. 박싱데이에는 언제나 상점이 쇼핑객으로 가득 찬다. 때때로 사람들은 상점이 문을 열기 전에 매장 밖에서 기다리기도 한다. 그들은 상품을 가장 저렴한 가격에 구매할 좋은 기회를 얻는다. 그들은 값싼 텔레비전이나 옷, 가구를 구매하고 싶어 한다. 하지만, 박싱데이는 사람들을 다소 미치게 하기도 한다. 그들은 일단 상점에 발을 들여놓으면 마구 돌아다니면서 닥치는 대로 물건을 집는다. 심지어 그들은 물건을 놓고 싸움을 벌이기도 한다! 박싱데이에는 고객들이 몰리거나, 다치거나, 심지어 죽을 가능성도 있다. 고객들을 보호하기 위해서 상점은 흔히 입장객 수를 제한하기도 한다.

| 문제 해설 |

1 윗글은 박싱데이에 일어날 수 있는 일을 묘사하고 있다.
① 박싱데이의 기원
② 싼 물건을 살 수 있는 장소
③ 박싱데이의 특별한 모습들
④ 가장 많은 수입을 얻는 방법
⑤ 크리스마스와 박싱데이의 관계

2 사람들이 상점에서 벌이는 거친 행동을 묘사한 문장이 나오기 전인 ⓒ가 가장 적절하다.
하지만, 박싱데이는 사람들을 다소 미치게 하기도 한다.

3 최상의 가격(the best price)이라는 뜻은 소비자에게 있어서 최상의 가격을 말하므로 가장 싼 가격을 의미한다. 가장 싼 가격에 물건을 살 수 있으므로 가장 많은 손님이 상점을 찾아올 것이다.
사람들은 박싱데이에 회사가 가장 싼 가격으로 상품을 판매한다고 생각한다. 그래서 상점에는 일 년 중 (이날에) 손님이 가장 많다.

4 상점은 손님을 보호하려고 (in order to protect customers) 상점에 들어오는 손님의 수를 제한한다.

| 영영풀이 |

1 generate: 산출하다
2 potential: 잠재성, 가능성
3 fatality: 죽음

| 구문풀이 |

3행 They often sell their products at **highly discounted** *prices*.
highly는 '대단히, 매우'라는 뜻으로 discounted를 수식하고 highly discounted는 prices를 수식한다.

8행 Once inside, they often rush around and grab **whatever** they can.
Once와 inside 사이에 they go가 생략되었다고 볼 수 있다. whatever는 선행사를 포함하는 복합 관계대명사로 anything that으로 바꿔 쓸 수 있다. they can 다음에 grab이 생략되었다고 보면 이해하기 쉽다. (~ grab anything that they can grab)

11행 they often limit the number of *people* **who** are allowed inside
who는 선행사 people을 수식하는 주격 관계대명사절을 이끈다.

03 | SPACE p.73

1 ④ 2 ② 3 ④
4 Earth, Mars

요즘에는 지구에 질병, 오염, 전쟁이 많이 발생해서, 언젠가는 인간이 다른 행성에서 살게 될지도 모른다고 사람들은 생각한다. 그러나 대부분의 행성들은 지구의 적도 지역보다 덥거나, 남극이나 북극보다 더 추운가 하면 사람이 가서 살기에는 너무 멀리 떨어져 있다.
하지만 많은 과학자들이 화성은 사람들이 미래에 살 수 있는 행성일지도 모른다고 생각한다. 화성까지 가려면 시간이 오래 걸리겠지만, 그래도 지구에서 가장 가까운 행성이다. 얼마 전에 미국은 화성에 물이 있는지 조사하려고 우주선을 보냈다. 이제 화성에 물이 존재한다는 것이 밝혀졌다. 물이 있다면 인간이 그곳에서 사는 것도 가능할 것이다. 인간이 사는 데는 물이 필요하고, 또 물은 지구로 돌아오는 데 필요한 연료를 만드는 데 사용될 수도 있기 때문에 이 사실은 중요한 것이다. 그러나 화성에는 바람이 너무 강하고 산소가 충분하지 않을 수 있어서 사람이 사는 것이 어려울 수도 있다. 그래도 언젠가 곧 화성에 가고 싶은가?

| 문제 해설 |

1 많은 과학자들이 사람들이 살 수 있는 행성으로 화성을 지목하고 있다는 점을 언급한 뒤, 화성에서 물이 발견되었다는 점을 언급하고 있으므로, 이 글의 목적으로 적절한 것은 ④이다.
① 지구와 화성을 비교하기 위해
② 사람들에게 환경 오염에 대해 경고하기 위해
③ 우리가 더 이상 지구에서 못 사는 이유를 설명하기 위해
④ 미래에 화성에서 살 가능성에 대해 설명하기 위해
⑤ 독자에게 되도록 빨리 화성에 가야 한다고 설득하기 위해

2 다음 문장에서 화성에 물이 존재한다는 것이 밝혀졌다는 내용이 나오므로 미국이 우주선을 보낸 목적이 물이 있는지 조사하기 위함임을 알 수 있다.
① 아무도 모르게
② 물을 찾기 위해
③ 온도를 확인하기 위해
④ 최초로 그리고 그것과 교신이 끊겼다
⑤ 생물이 있는지 찾기 위해

3 대부분의 행성이 지구보다 훨씬 덥거나 춥다고 말하고는 있지만 '화성이 지구보다 훨씬 춥다'고 직접적으로 언급하지 않았다.
① 화성은 지구와 가장 가까운 행성이다.
② 화성은 바람이 너무 많다.
③ 화성에 물이 있다.
④ 화성은 지구보다 훨씬 춥다.
⑤ 화성은 산소가 충분하지 않다.

4 지구에는 문제가 많다. 사람들은 지구를 떠나 다른 행성에서 살지도 모른다. 그러나 대부분의 행성들은 너무 덥거나, 춥거나, 사람들이 가기에는 너무 멀리 떨어져 있다. 화성은 지구에서 가장 가까운 행성이다. 화성에 물이 있기 때문에 사람들은 그곳에서 살 수 있을 것이다.

| 영영풀이 |

1 pollution: 오염
2 prove: 증명하다
3 fuel: 연료

| 구문풀이 |

2행 Most planets are hotter than the places on the Earth's equator, colder than the Earth's north or south poles, or too far away for people to live.
이 문장은 「주어+be동사+보어」 구조로 된 2형식이다. 보어 부분은 hotter ~ equator, colder ~ south poles, too far away ~ to live가 등위접속사 or를 통해 병렬로 연결되었다.

9행 If there is water, then **it** might be possible for humans **to live there**.
it은 가주어, to live there는 진주어이며, for humans는 to부정사의 의미상 주어이다.

11행 Mars can have too much wind and not enough oxygen, **which** might make **it** difficult *for people* **to live there**.
which는 앞 절 전체를 받는 관계대명사 계속적 용법이다. 이 관계대명사절은 앞 절 내용을 부연설명한다. 관계사절 안은 가목적어-진목적어(to부정사)가 쓰인 구조이다. for people은 to부정사의 의미상 주어이다.

Review Test p.74

A

1 pollution 2 figure
3 fuel 4 generate
5 accustomed

B

1 ③ 2 ② 3 ④

C

1 They used not only direct but reflected light to depict nature objectively.
2 Once inside, they often rush around and grab whatever they can.
3 Many scientists think that Mars might be a planet where people could live in the future.

A

1 pollution: 오염
2 figure: 인물
3 fuel: 연료
4 generate: 산출하다
5 accustomed: 익숙해진

B

1 originate: 비롯되다, 유래하다(= start)
가장 초기의 유리잔은 고대 이집트에서 시작되었다.
2 product: 제품, 상품(= goods)
2층에서는 유럽에서 온 값비싼 제품을 볼 수 있습니다.
3 prove: 증명하다(= demonstrate)
이 새 약이 효과적이라는 것은 아직 증명되지 않았다.

C

1 not only A but also B: A뿐만 아니라 B도
2 Once inside (= Once they are inside)
whatever they can = anything that they can
3 a planet: 선행사
where(= on the planet) people could live in the future: 관계부사절

01 | PLACES p.77

1 ⑤ 2 ② 3 화재, 불법 이민자

영불 해저 터널은 세계에서 가장 놀라운 기술적 성과 중 하나다. '처널(영불 해저 터널)'로 알려진 이 터널은 영국과 프랑스 사이에서 운행되고 있다. 이 터널은 영국 해협 아래에 건설되어 있다. 사실 이 터널은 세계에서 가장 긴 해저 터널이다. 이 터널은 유럽과 영국제도 사이를 더 쉽게 이동하기 위해 구상되었다. 영국과 프랑스 사이의 해저 터널에 대한 아이디어는 원래 1802년에 처음 제안되었다. 하지만, 그 프로젝트에 대한 공사가 추진되기 시작한 것은 겨우 1980년대가 되어서였다. 드디어 1994년에 처널이 공식적으로 개통되었다. 이 터널은 개통 이후부터 몇 가지 문제점이 노출되었다. 몇 건의 작은 화재가 일어나 터널 서비스가 중단되었다. 초기에는 영국으로 들어오는 불법 이주자 문제도 있었다. 하지만, 이 두 가지 문제는 철저히 조사되고 있고, 터널의 긴급 출동 요원은 어떠한 상황도 처리할 수 있도록 잘 훈련되어 있다.

| 문제 해설 |

1 어떤 상황도 처리할 수 있는 잘 훈련된 응급 요원들이 터널 안에 있다고 했으므로 ⑤가 정답이다.
① 영국인들이 해저 터널에 관한 의견을 제안했다.
② 초기 처널의 목적은 상품을 운반하는 것이었다.
③ 처널을 짓는 데 약 백 년이 걸렸다.
④ 불법 이민자의 문제가 아직도 존재한다.
⑤ 문제를 처리할 수 있는 긴급 출동 요원이 터널에 배치되어 있다.

2 처음으로 터널에 관련된 의견이 제안되었다는 내용이 나온 문장과 터널이 완공되었다는 내용이 나온 문장 사이인 ⓑ가 가장 적절하다.
하지만, 그 프로젝트에 대한 공사가 추진되기 시작한 것은 겨우 1980년대가 되어서였다.

3 several small fires와 illegal immigrants가 some problems에 해당한다.

| 영영풀이 |

1 feat: 위업
2 initially: 처음에
3 thoroughly: 철저히

| 구문풀이 |

2행 **Known** as "The Chunnel," it operates between Great Britain and France.
Known as "The Chunnel,"은 분사구문으로 Known 앞에 Being이 생략되어 있다.

4행 It was designed to **make** travel from Europe to the British Isles easier. (O / OC)
make+O+OC: ~을 …하게 만들다

9행 there was also a problem with *illegal immigrants* **entering** Britain
entering Britain이 illegal immigrants를 뒤에서 수식하고 있다.

10행 **both of these issues** have been examined thoroughly
「both of+복수명사」는 '~ 둘 다'라는 뜻이고, 복수동사로 받는다.

02 | TRAGEDY p.79

1 ②
2 ⓐ had suffered from ⓑ consisted of
3 ④
4 misuse of medication administered by his personal physician

팝의 제왕은 누구인가? 마이클 잭슨이다! 그는 뮤직비디오와 작곡, 라이브 콘서트로 음악의 혁명을 일으켰다. 마이클 잭슨의 음악 경력은 아주 어릴 적부터 시작되었다.
(B) 그는 잭슨 파이브의 리드 싱어가 되었을 때 겨우 여덟 살이었다. 잭슨 파이브는 마이클과 그의 형제들로 구성되어 있었다. 드디어 마이클은 솔로 활동을 시작했다. 그리고 1980년대 초에 팝의 제왕이 되었다. 그는 시대를 통틀어 가장 인기 있는 노래 몇 곡을 썼다. 〈빌리 진〉과 〈스릴러〉 같은 노래는 그를 음악계의 슈퍼스타로 만들어 주는 데 일조했다.
(A) 하지만, 2009년 6월 25일, 이 팝스타의 죽음이 전 세계에 충격을 안겨주었다. 그는 심장 마비로 고통을 겪은 적이 있었다. 마이클은 사망 당시 몇 가지 다른 약물을 복용하고 있었다. 거기에는 몇 가지 종류의 진통제가 포함되어 있었다. 의사들은 주치의에 의해 처방된 약의 오용이 그의 때 이른 죽음에 한몫을 했을 거라고 말했다.
(C) 전 세계 수백만 명의 팬들이 사랑과 지지를 보여주었다. 그들은 마이클을 기려 기념비를 세우고 그의 노래를 함께 불렀다. 그에 대한 기억은 잊을 수 없는 그의 음악을 통해 영원히 살아 있을 것이다.

| 문제 해설 |

1 마이클 잭슨의 일대기를 다룬 내용이다. (B) 음악을 시작해서 전성기에 이르는 내용 → (A) 갑작스러운 죽음에 관련된 내용 → (C) 팬들의 애도에 관련된 내용의 순서가 적절하다.

2 ⓐ 마이클 잭슨의 죽음이 과거의 일이므로 과거(마이클 잭슨의 죽음)보다 먼저 일어난 일은 대과거인 과거완료로 써야 한다. ⓑ consist of가 '~로 이루어져 있다, ~로 되어 있다'라는 뜻이므로 능동태로 써야 한다.

3 수를 세는 단위에 's'가 붙어서 '수백만의'라는 의미가 되므로 '수백만 명의 팬들이'라고 해석해야 한다. '백만 명의 팬'은 one million fans라고 쓴다.

4 의사들에 따르면 마이클 잭슨의 죽음이 그의 주치의에 의해 투약된 약물의 잘못된 사용 때문일 것이라고 말했다.
마이클 잭슨의 죽음의 원인은 무엇인가?

| 영영풀이 |

1 live: 라이브의
2 suffer: 고통받다
3 administer: (약을) 투여하다

| 구문풀이 |

9행 Doctors said **that** misuse of medication administered by his personal physician **played a role** in his **untimely death**.

that은 said의 목적어절을 이끄는 종속접속사이다. play a role은 '한몫하다, 중요한 역할을 하다'라는 의미이고, untimely death는 '요절', 즉 '때 이른 죽음'을 의미한다.

15행 Songs [**such as** *Billie Jean* and *Thriller*] **helped** (to) **make** him a musical superstar.

such as는 '예를 들어, 이를테면 ~과 같은'이라는 뜻이다. Songs가 주어이고 helped가 동사이다. help 뒤에는 to부정사, 원형부정사 둘 다 올 수 있다.
make+O+OC: ~가 …하도록 만들다
목적격 보어(a musical superstar)가 명사(구)이므로 목적어(him)과 동일함을 의미한다.

03 | WORLD NEWS p.81

1 ② 2 ① 3 ⑤
4 modern, Bible, communities

아미시인들은 누구인가? 아미시인들은 약 14만 명으로, 미국의 펜실베이니아 주의 랭커스터 군이나 캐나다의 온타리오 주 같은 곳에서 살고 있다. 아미시인들은 현대 문화를 거부하고, 자신의 생활양식을 종교에 귀착시켜 생활하는 것으로 유명하다. 그 사람들은 성경에 있는 것을 문자 그대로 믿는다. 또 큰 사회와는 격리된 채 생활해야 된다고 믿는다.
그들의 생활양식은 다른 현대인들과는 다르다. 아미시 남성들은 검은 양복을 입고, 검은 구두를 신으며, 밀짚으로 만든 챙이 넓은 모자를 쓴다. 여성들은 단색 드레스에다 망토와 앞치마를 걸치고 다닌다. 자녀를 일곱이나 여덟 명 낳는 아미시 부부가 많다. 아미시 어린이들은 8학년을 마칠 때까지만 학교에 다닌다. 그 사람들은 현대의 기술 때문에 인간 생활이 향상된다고 생각하지 않는다.
최근에는 아미시인들이 사는 곳을 찾아가 그 사람들의 특이한 생활양식을 구경하는 관광객들이 많아졌다.

| 문제 해설 |

1 그들(아미시)의 생활양식은 다른 현대인들과는 다르다는 내용 뒤에 아미시가 어떻게 다른지 구체적으로 설명하는 내용이 나와야 자연스럽다.

2 아미시 사람들은 성경에 있는 것을 문자 그대로 믿고 사회와 격리된 채 살아야 한다고 믿으므로 pious(독실한)가 옳다.
① 독실한
② 세속적인
③ 이기적인
④ 문명화된
⑤ 비관적인

3 They believe that they should keep themselves away from the larger society.를 통해 그들은 더 큰 사회와 격리된 채 생활해야 된다고 믿는다는 것을 알 수 있으므로 아미시인들이 관광객들과 의사소통을 하려고 외국어를 배운다는 것은 짐작할 수 없다.
① 도시에서 떨어진 시골에서 살기를 좋아한다.
② 여성들은 단색 옷을 입는다.
③ 남성들은 검정색 신발을 신는다.
④ 어린이들은 8학년 이후 학교에 가지 않는다.
⑤ 관광객과 대화를 나누기 위해 외국어를 공부한다.

4 아미시인들은 현대 문화를 거부한 채 다른 사람들과는 다르게 사는 사람들이다. 그 사람들은 성경에 쓰여 있는 모든 것을 믿으며, 큰 사회와는 격리되어 생활해야 된다고 생각한다. 그 사람들의 독특한 생활양식 때문에 아미시인들이 사는 곳을 찾아와 특이한 생활을 구경하는 관광객들이 많다.

| 영영풀이 |

1 improve: 개선하다, 향상시키다

2 observe: 관찰하다

3 differ: 다르다

| 구문풀이 |

2행 The Amish are famous for **rejecting** modern culture and **keeping** their lifestyle tied into their religion.

rejecting과 keeping은 각각 for의 목적어로 만들어주기 위해 동명사 형태로 고친 것이다. keeping their lifestyle tied into their religion 부분은 「keep+목적어+목적격 보어(p.p.)」 형식으로 되어있다.

4행 They believe literally everything **written in the Bible**.

written in the Bible은 everything을 수식하는 분사구이고, written 앞에 「관계대명사+be동사」가 생략되었다.

9행 Amish people don't think the modern technology **helps** (to) improve human lives.

help는 to부정사, 원형부정사 둘 다 목적어로 취할 수 있다.

Review Test p.82

A

1 live 2 suffer

3 feat 4 thoroughly

5 improve

B

1 ⑤ 2 ④ 3 ⑤

C

1 It was only in the 1980s that construction began on the project.

2 He was only eight years old when he became the lead singer of the Jackson 5.

3 The Amish are famous for rejecting modern culture and keeping their lifestyle tied into their religion.

A

1 live: 라이브의

2 suffer: 고통받다

3 feat: 위업

4 thoroughly: 철저히

5 improve: 개선하다, 향상시키다

B

1 handle: 다루다, 처리하다(= deal with)
저 혼자 이 문제들을 처리할 수 있으니 걱정하지 마세요.

2 untimely: 때 아닌, 때 이른(= early)
모두가 그의 요절 소식에 충격을 받았다.

3 observe: 관찰하다(= watch)
그 운 좋은 방문객들은 수족관에서 고래가 새끼를 낳는 모습을 볼 수 있었다.

C

1 It ~ that 강조구문 (only in the 1980s 강조)

2 when 주어+동사: ~할 때 (when: 시간 부사절 접속사)

3 be famous for: ~로 유명하다
rejecting modern culture, keeping their lifestyle ~: 전치사 for의 목적어

01 | CAMPAIGN p.85

1 ③ 2 ①

3 The, warmer, the, more

4 ④

2월 27일이 국제 북극곰의 날이라는 것을 알고 있는가? 북극곰은 기후 변화 때문에 가장 먼저 멸종 위기에 처한 종이었다. 기후가 따뜻해지면 질수록, 북극의 얼음이 더 많이 녹게 될 것이다. 이는 북극곰의 서식지와 생존에 심각한 위협을 내포한다. 북극곰을 보호하는 것을 돕고 싶다면, 당신이 이바지할 수 있는 방법이 아주 많다. 현재 북극곰을 구하는 데 헌신하는 몇몇 조직이 있다. 여기에는 미국야생동식물연맹과 북극곰 인터내셔널이 포함되어 있다. (북극곰은 육식동물이고 대부분은 물개를 잡아먹는다.) 이들 단체의 각각의 기부금은 북극곰을 구하는 데 쓰일 것이다. 또한, 에너지를 아끼려고 노력함으로써, 그리고 탄소 발자국을 줄이려고 대중교통을 이용함으로써 (북극곰을) 도울 수도 있다. 지구 온난화를 늦추는 것이 북극곰의 자연 서식지를 보존하는 데 도움이 될 것이다. 가장 작은 변화조차도 큰 차이를 만들 수 있다!

| 문제 해설 |

1 윗글은 북극곰을 돕는 방법에 대해 설명하고 있다.
① 북극곰이 먹는 것
② 북극곰이 사는 곳
③ 북극곰을 돕는 방법
④ 국제 북극곰의 날
⑤ 탄소 발자국을 줄이는 방법

2 (A) climate change가 명사(구)이므로 전치사인 because of가 와야 한다. (B) several organizations가 주어로 복수이므로 are가 와야 한다. (C) Each monetary donation이 북극곰을 구하는 데 쓰이는 것이므로 수동형인 will be put이 와야 한다.

3 '~하면 할수록, 점점 더 …하다'라는 표현은 「the+비교급+S+V, the+비교급+S+V」를 사용한다.
기후가 따뜻해지면 질수록, 북극의 얼음이 더 많이 녹게 될 것이다.

4 윗글은 북극곰을 보호하는 방법에 대한 것으로, 북극곰의 식습관에 대한 내용은 전체 내용과 맞지 않는다.

| 영영풀이 |

1 donation: 기부금
2 preserve: ~을 지키다, 보존하다
3 habitat: 서식지

| 구문풀이 |

5행 There are currently *several organizations* **dedicated to** saving the polar bear.
dedicated to는 '~에 전념하는, 헌신하는'이라는 뜻이고, dedicated 이하가 several organizations를 뒤에서 수식해 주고 있다. to는 전치사이기 때문에 saving이라는 동명사가 왔다.

7행 Polar bears are carnivorous, **mostly eating seals.**
mostly eating seals는 부대상황을 의미하는 분사구문으로 and they mostly eat seals로 바꿔 쓸 수 있다.

10행 You can also help **by making** an effort to conserve energy and **by using** public transportation **to reduce** your carbon footprint.
「by making ~ to conserve energy」와 「by using ~ carbon footprint」가 help에 병렬 연결된 구조이다. '~하기 위해 … 함으로써 도와줄 수 있다.'라고 해석하며, to conserve와 to reduce는 각각 in order to conserve와 in order to reduce로 바꿔 쓸 수 있다.

02 | FUTURE LIFE p.87

1 ③ 2 ④ 3 ③

4 장기간에 걸쳐서 유전자 변형 식품의 영향을 실험한 것이 없어서

오늘날의 과학자들은 진정으로 놀라운 것을 이뤄낼 수 있는 능력을 지니고 있다. 그들이 우리의 식품을 유전적으로 변화시킬 수 있다는 것을 알고 있었는가? 그것은 사실이다. 과거에는 농부들이 농작물을 재배하기 위해 전통적인 재배 기술을 사용했다. 그들은 자신들의 가장 우수한 곡물에서 종자를 수확함으로써 이를 행했다. 그런 다음, 그들은 이듬해에 이 종자를 심었다. 이 방법은 곡물의 질과 양을 개선하기 위해 사용되는데 이종교배라고 불린다. 가장 좋은 곡물에서 고른 것이라도 이러한 재배 방법은 많은 한계를 지니고 있었다. 과학자들은 이러한 한계를 극복하는 방법을 발견했다. 그들은 곡물이 박테리아와 바이러스, 해충에 더 잘 저항할 수 있도록 곡물을 변형할 수 있다. 이는 농부들이 자기들의 곡물을 보호하기 위해 사용하는 살충제의 양을 줄이는 데 도움을 준다. 게다가 변형된 종자는 농부들이 더 많은 양의 곡물을 생산하는 데 도움이 될 수 있다. 하지만, 부정적인 면도 있다. 예를 들어 유전자 변형 식품이 정말로 안전한지는 아무도 모른다. 유전자 변형 식품의 장기적 영향을 시험해보기 위해 고안된 실험은 없었다.

| 문제 해설 |

1 ①, ②, ④, ⑤는 farmers를 가리키고, ③은 seeds를 가리킨다.

2 박테리아와 바이러스, 병균에 저항력이 강한 곡식을 만들어서 더 많은 양의 곡식을 생산해 낼 수 있도록 돕는다는 내용이 되어야 한다.
① ~에 더 상처받기 쉬운 … 최고의
② ~에 더 수용하기 쉬운 … 더 이상한
③ ~에 면역성이 덜한 … 알려지지 않은 어떤
④ ~에 더 저항력이 있는 … 더 많은 양의
⑤ ~에 약함이 덜한 … 더 적은 양의

3 유전자 변형 식품의 단점이 나오기 시작하는 문장 앞인 ⓒ가 가장 자연스럽다.
하지만, 부정적인 면도 있다.

4 There have not been any experiments designed to test the long-term effects of genetically modified food.라는 문장에서 유전자 변형 식품의 영향을 장기간 실험해 본 결과가 없어서 안전성을 믿을 수 없음을 알 수 있다.

| 영영풀이 |

1 modify: ~을 변경[변형]하다
2 breed: 번식시키다, 품종 개량을 하다
3 method: 방법

| 구문풀이 |

5행 They **would** do this by harvesting seeds from their best crops.
would는 과거의 반복적인 행동을 나타내며, used to로 바꿔 쓸 수 있다. 과거의 상태를 나타낼 때는 would를 쓸 수 없다.
e.g.) (O) There used to be an apple tree next to my house.
우리 집 옆에 사과나무가 있었다.
(X) There would be an apple tree next to my house.

6행 *This method*, **which** is used to improve the quality and the quantity of crops, is called hybridization.
which는 선행사 This method를 받는 계속적 용법의 주격 관계대명사이다.

11행 This helps to reduce the quantity of *pesticides* farmers use to protect their crops.
pesticides와 farmers 사이에 pesticides를 선행사로 받으면서, use의 목적어가 되는 목적격 관계대명사가 생략되어 있다.

12행 modifying seeds can **help** them produce a larger quantity of crops
help는 목적격 보어로 동사원형이나 to부정사를 취하고, '~가 …하는 것을 돕다'라고 해석한다.

13행 **nobody** knows how(의문사) safe(형용사) genetically modified food(주어) really is(동사)
nobody는 전체 부정을 나타내는 부정대명사로 '아무도 ~ 않다'라고 해석한다.
의문사 how는 형용사/부사와 함께 쓰여, '얼마나 ~한(하게)'로 해석할 수 있고, 이와 같은 간접의문문에서는 「동사+주어」가 아닌 「주어+동사」의 어순을 따른다.

03 | HISTORY p.89

1 ① 2 ④

3 Americans thought buying Alaska was a big mistake and waste of money. They named it after William H. Seward, who insisted the purchase.

4 Russia, gold, the Alaska Statehood Act, the forty-ninth state

미국은 1867년에 러시아에 7백만 달러를 주고 알래스카를 샀다. 미국인들은 대부분 이것은 큰 실수이며 돈 낭비라고 생각했다. 그래서 알래스카를 "수어드의 바보짓"이라느니, "수어드의 아이스박스"라고 불렀다. 당시 미국의 국무부 장관으로, 알래스카의 매입을 주장했던 윌리엄 H. 수어드의 이름을 따서 그렇게 불렀던 것이다.
그러나 1896년에서 1902년 사이에 그곳에서 금이 발견되었고, 거의 하룻밤 사이에 알래스카의 도시들이 모두 우후죽순 격으로 생겨났다. 그때쯤에는 벌써 알래스카 주민들은 주로 승격시켜 달라고 싸웠지만, 정부는 그 요구를 무시했다. 제2차 세계대전이 벌어지고 있던 1941년에 미국이 일본에 선전포고를 하게 되자, 알래스카는 그 전략적 위치 때문에 상당히 중요해졌다. 그래서 미국 정부는 알래스카를 주로 승격시키는 문제를 진지하게 고려하기 시작했다.
알래스카 주민들은 대표단을 선출해 아이젠하워 대통령과 면담을 추진했다. 이 대표단은 대통령을 설득해 1958년에 알래스카 주 승격 법안에 서명하도록 만들었다. 드디어 1959년 1월 3일에 알래스카는 미국의 49번째 주가 되었다.

| 문제 해설 |

1 윗글은 미국이 러시아에게 알래스카를 매입하고 49번째 주로 승격한 내용을 다루고 있으므로 ①의 '미국의 49번 째 주가 된 알래스카'가 주제로 적절하다.
① 미국의 49번째 주가 된 알래스카
② 알래스카 매입
③ 알래스카의 금 발견
④ 알래스카의 경제와 주민들
⑤ 아이젠하워 대통령과의 만남

2 제2차 세계대전 중 미국이 일본에게 선전포고를 하고 알래스카가 전략적 요충지가 되어서 미국 정부가 알래스카를 주로 승격시키는 문제를 진지하게 고려하고 있었으므로 아이젠하워 대통령은 대표단과 만나기 전에 알래스카 주 승격 법안에 서명할 것을 고려하고 있었다는 것을 추론할 수 있다.

① 아이젠하워는 알래스카가 러시아의 주였을 때 그곳에서 태어났다.
② 아이젠하워는 늘 알래스카 주 승격 법안에 서명하고 싶었다.
③ 아이젠하워는 알래스카 주 승격 법안 서명 이전에 사임했다.
④ 아이젠하워는 대표단을 만나기 전에 알래스카 주 승격 법안 서명을 고려하고 있었다.
⑤ 아이젠하워는 제2차 세계대전 동안 러시아 군대와 함께 일본을 침략하려고 노력했다.

3 미국인들은 알래스카 매입이 큰 실수이고 돈 낭비라고 생각해서, 그 매입을 추진한 수어드의 이름을 붙였다.

4 미국은 1867년 러시아로부터 알래스카를 매입했다. 몇 년 후 알래스카에서 금이 발견되었고, 제2차 세계대전 중 알래스카는 전략적으로 중요한 장소가 되었다. 이와 같은 이유로, 미국 정부는 알래스카를 49번째 주로 만들기로 결정했다. 마침내, 아이젠하워 대통령은 1958년에 알래스카 주 승격 법안에 서명하고, 알래스카는 1959년에 미국의 49번째 주가 되었다.

| 영영풀이 |

1 insist: 주장하다
2 ignore: 무시하다
3 convince: 확신시키다, 설득하다

| 구문풀이 |

3행 They named it after William H. Seward, the Secretary of State of the United States, **who insisted the purchase**.

who insisted the purchase는 William H. Seward를 부연설명하는 계속적 용법의 관계대명사절이다. the Secretary of State of the United States는 William H. Seward와 동격이다.

10행 They **convinced** him to sign the Alaska Statehood Act in 1958.

convince+목적어+to부정사: ~가 ...하도록 설득하다

Review Test p.90

A

1 donation
2 ignore
3 modify
4 method
5 convince

B

1 ④
2 ②
3 ②

C

1 There are currently several organizations dedicated to saving the polar bear.
2 For instance, nobody knows how safe genetically modified food really is.
3 They named it after William H. Seward, who insisted the purchase.

A

1 donation: 기부금
2 ignore: 무시하다
3 modify: ~을 변경[변형]하다
4 method: 방법
5 convince: 확신시키다, 설득하다

B

1 conserve: 아끼다, 보호하다(= preserve)
우리는 우리 자손들을 위해 열대우림을 보호해야 한다.
2 downside: 불리한 면, 단점(= drawback)
그 정책의 단점은 시행 비용이 너무 비싸다는 점이다.
3 delegate: 대표, 사절(= representative)
101개국의 대표단들이 그 국제 행사에 참가했다.

C

1 (that are) dedicated to saving the polar bear: several organizations 수식
2 간접의문문 어순: 의문사+주어+동사
3 name A after B: B의 이름을 따서 A의 이름을 붙이다

Workbook

Unit 01 p.92

A

1 features
2 distance
3 peak
4 mass-produce
5 influential

B ②

C

Unit 01-02

influential artists, drawing pictures, fine art, best known artwork, painted celebrities, mass-produce their artwork, making copies, making money, believed in

Unit 01-03

seas and oceans, blue light, to appear blue, made up of, the wavelength, about half that, nearly ten times, in detail

Unit 02 p.94

A

1 enormous
2 distracted
3 thrived
4 rejected
5 indigenous

B ③

C

Unit 02-01

built in 1624, during his reign, demonstrated the vast wealth, taking responsibility, any interference from them, maintain the palace, serving the king, national income

Unit 02-03

servants and slaves, possessions, his nephew, take good care of, Everything else, faithful to me, thoughtfully, nothing from him, some meaning, the head slave

Unit 03 p.96

A

1 emerge
2 repetitive
3 observe
4 face
5 threat

B ⑤

C

Unit 03-02

survived many battles, die in combat, the service, passed away, memorial service, somber holiday, sacrificed their lives, mark the occasion, in defense of, observed nationwide

Unit 03-03

have hunted, were used to, good luck charm, used them, short knives, in medicines, the threat of extinction

Unit 04 p.98

A

1 administrative
2 relinquish
3 autonomy
4 identified
5 innocent

B ⑤

C

Unit 04-01

special administrative region, has existed, their colony, trading outpost, open important trade relations, overseas province, return the colony, relinquish control, high degree of autonomy

Unit 04-02

what happened, were hijacked, on board, was flown, overpower the hijackers, glued to, was identified, war on terrorism, innocent people, anger and sadness, In an effort to, where, not only, but also

Unit 05 p.100

A

1 belongs
2 passenger
3 afford
4 Average
5 majority

B ③

C

Unit 05-01

complain about problems, on a daily basis, try to fix them, break a bad habit, the same wrist, onto your other wrist, might feel better

Unit 05-03

are disappearing, only that language, endangered minority cultures, following generations, their languages are lost, face extinction, at a rate of, What contributes, discrimination, starvation, pass on, better opportunity

Unit 06 p.102

A

1 decorated
2 declared
3 inspired
4 sponsored
5 concern

B ①

C

Unit 06-01

few of them, For seven days, ice sculptures, historical events, design their sculptures, are illuminated with, dine on, three hundred statues

Unit 06-03

teenage smokers, a serious level, big influences, peer pressure, they are curious, celebrities, behave, the earlier, the more difficult, regular smokers, as a result of

Unit 07 p.104

A

1 determine
2 launched
3 glacial
4 normal
5 declined

B ②

C

Unit 07-02

face-to-face, now extinct, inhabited the Earth, weighed, roam, started to decline, the few remaining specimens, climate change, began to melt, natural habitat, human activity, humans hunting wooly mammoths

Unit 07-03

ozone layer, less than normal, the ultraviolet light, cause cancers, certain gases we release, car air conditioning systems, fire extinguishers, less products

Unit 08 p.106

A

1 equator
2 purchased
3 revenue
4 landscape
5 depicting

B ②

C

Unit 08-01

originated in France, significant departure, in the center, changed the old belief, outdoor scenes, depict nature objectively, accustomed to seeing, Anybody could be painted, a bartender

Unit 08-03

another planet, north or south poles, take a long time, the closest planet, there is water, for humans to live, to make fuel, too much wind

Unit 09 p.108

A

1 operating
2 immigrant
3 underneath
4 untimely
5 differs

B ⑤

C

Unit 09-02

revolutionized music, very early age, the lead singer, consisted of, most popular music, pop star's death, cardiac arrest, painkillers, misuse of medication, played a role, in honor of, live on

Unit 09-03

population, rejecting modern culture, tied into their religion, literally, keep themselves away, differs from, cape and apron, seven or eight, the eighth grade, improve human lives, singular way

Unit 10 p.110

A

1 numerous
2 named
3 elected
4 strategic
5 effort

B ⑤

C

Unit 10-02

ability to achieve, genetically modify, breeding techniques, best crops, improve the quality, hybridization, many limits, more resistant, pesticides, how safe, long-term effects

Unit 10-03

waste of money, named it after, insisted, gold was discovered, overnight, the statehood, strategic position, seriously consider, forty-ninth state